PUBLIC PARTICIPATION IN URBAN DEVELOPMENT

TO BE
DISPOSED
BY
AUTHORITY

The Policy Studies Institute (PSI) is Britain's leading independent research organisation undertaking studies of economic, industrial and social policy, and the workings of political institutions.

PSI is a registered charity, run on a non-profit basis, and is not associated with any political party, pressure group or commercial interest.

PSI attaches great importance to covering a wide range of subject areas with its multi-disciplinary approach. The Institute's researchers are organised in groups which currently cover the following programmes:

Crime, Justice and Youth Studies – Employment and Society – Ethnic Equality and Diversity – European Industrial Development – Family Finances – Information and Citizenship – Information and Cultural Studies – Social Care and Health Studies – Work, Benefits and Social Participation

This publication arises from the European Industrial Development group and is one of over 30 publications made available by the Institute each year.

Information about the work of PSI and a catalogue of available books can be obtained from:

Marketing Department, PSI
100 Park Village East, London NW1 3SR

Public Participation in Urban Development

The European Experience

James Barlow

POLICY STUDIES INSTITUTE
London

The publishing imprint of the independent
POLICY STUDIES INSTITUTE
100 Park Village East, London NW1 3SR
Telephone: 0171-387 2171   Fax: 0171-388 0914

© Policy Studies Institute 1995

ISBN 0 85374 644 3

PSI Research Report 777

A CIP catalogue record of this book is available from the British Library.

1 2 3 4 5 6 7 8 9

PSI publications are available from
BEBC Distribution Ltd
P O Box 1496, Poole, Dorset, BH12 3YD

Books will normally be despatched within 24 hours. Cheques should be made payable to BEBC Distribution Ltd.

Credit card and telephone/fax orders may be placed on the following freephone numbers:

FREEPHONE: 0800 262260
FREEFAX: 0800 262266

Booktrade representation (UK & Eire):
Broadcast Books
24 De Montfort Road, London SW16 1LW
Telephone: 0181-677 5129

PSI subscriptions are available from PSI's subscription agent
Carfax Publishing Company Ltd
P O Box 25, Abingdon, Oxford OX14 3UE

Laserset by Policy Studies Institute
Printed at Redwood Books, Trowbridge, Wiltshire.

Contents

Preface

The background to this report

The government is attempting to make the planning system more accessible and easier to use. Since July 1992 it has been a statutory requirement for English and Welsh local authorities to publicise all planning applications so that all interested parties can make their views known. The Department of the Environment has also recently given guidance to local planning authorities on the organisation and procedure of public local inquiries.[1] And, as a contribution to the 'Citizen's Charter', the DOE, the Welsh Office and the National Planning Forum have produced booklets to help the public better understand planning services.[2] This recently prompted the then minister for planning, David Curry, to claim:

> Everyone should now be able to find out easily how the planning system works and what a good standard of planning service involves – whether they are applying for planning permission themselves or commenting on a neighbour's plans or their council's development plan. It is important that the public should understand the planning system so they can get involved as much as possible.[3]

Ministers have given high priority to public inquiries into local plans,[4] but progress towards full coverage by adopted plans has been slower than expected. This is largely because the average duration of local plan inquiries has increased from ten to around forty weeks since 1989. The growing length of time spent on inquiries suggests there may be a link between increased awareness of the importance of local plans and greater participation.

There is, of course, a long tradition of debate on public participation and its role in local democracy; attempts to promote 'community' involvement in urban planning go back many years. The Town and Country Planning Act 1971 emphasised that adequate public participation should be a pre-condition for the approval of structure and local plans; several documents issued by the DOE subsequently set out practical guidelines for public involvement in the planning process.[5] However, the legal and administrative requirements were sufficiently flexible to be interpreted differently by each county council, and concern was frequently expressed about the effectiveness of methods for involving the public in the planning process.

Planning and participation in the 1980s

The current revival of interest in participation arrives on the back of more than a decade of reform to the British town and country planning system. Planning was transformed in the 1980s by a succession of Conservative governments, insisting first that it meet the challenge of the 'market' by 'rolling back' planning regulations and later that it embrace greater public participation. The effect of these changes was to increasingly expose the political nature of urban development; the interaction between the main groups involved in the urban development process – the state, public pressure groups, local residents, landowners, developers and other businesses – became more conflictual.

In the 1980s, central government saw participation as a barrier to effective planning and development (Smith et al 1986). The Local Government, Planning and Land Act 1980 replaced the requirement for consultation on matters to be included in plans with a requirement for publicity and participation only at the draft plan stage. Furthermore, a public inquiry was deemed to be no longer necessary if participants agreed to deal with objections in writing. During this period new forms of public-private relationship were also struck between developers, local and central government. In some areas an integral part of the urban development process involved quangos embracing developers, the business community, landowners and local authorities.

However, another feature of the 1980s was the rise in anti-development protest by local residents' groups. This has become known as 'nimby' – 'not in my backyard' – protest, but it should be emphasised that the term is often used pejoratively to question the motives of protesters who may have wide-ranging grievances. Nevertheless, the emergence of anti-development protest was particularly worrying to the government and to development interests. As the social composition of 'rural' and city-fringe areas altered, partly in response to the changing distribution of employment opportunities and availability of housing, pressure for housing development on 'greenfield' sites heightened nimby protest. This grew to such an extent that there was concern amongst Conservative Party activists that excessive development might undermine the Party's natural electoral base (Barlow and Savage 1986). One commentator (Sullivan 1985: 44) warned Conservatives that 'the image of a property developing, polluting government is likely to prove disastrous in an election'.

Conservative politicians were not the only group worried about the rising tide of nimbyism. In some cases the blurring of environmental and conservation issues with more parochial nimby protest increased the ability of protesters to rouse public and media support. This had a severe impact on developers. As a spokesman for Consortium Developments, a grouping of major housebuilders which failed to build a single house during its existence, put it: 'Our problem is that new settlements are a housing issue but they are being dressed up as green ones.'[6]

Given the increased 'politicisation' of urban development, it is perhaps not surprising that by the end of the 1980s the government should have become more interested in strengthening the planning system and finding ways of involving the public more closely in decision making.[7] Another factor behind the impetus for greater participation is the recognition that the planning process is a powerful tool for managing environmental change and promoting a more 'sustainable' society. This, however, raises questions about who establishes the values and sets the standards for such a society. Potter et al (1994) argue that it is not enough to urge planners to look to the public as *consumers* to supply the necessary valuations – when it comes to developing sustainable local plans, the *values* citizens hold as citizens should come before their preferences as consumers. Improvement in the methods by which the public participates in the planning process has become critical for a smooth-running development system.

The scope of this report
There has, as Nadin (1992) points out, been only limited research on participation in the planning process in the last decade or so. This largely comprises work on innovative practice in community planning at the local level (Best and Bowser 1986; Alty and Darke 1991), on the impact of participation in plan preparation (Alterman et al 1984; Smith et al 1986; Webster and Lavers 1991); and on formal procedures following the deposit of plans (Bruton et al 1982). Perhaps the most recent major study of public involvement in planning was research on representations made by different groups at local plan inquiries (Adams et al 1990; Adams and Pawson 1992). This draws conclusions on the need to expand access to local planning procedure and provide further support for planning advocacy.

Although questions of participation have been comparatively under-researched, there has been more interest in recent years in the broad politics of urban development. The concepts of 'growth coalitions' and 'urban regimes' have been influential in work on the changing relationships between the different parties involved in urban development. There has also been some research on 'nimbyism', but this has largely focused on neighbourhood protest over the provision of community care facilities (Gleeson and Memon 1994; Jaffe and Smith 1986), or protest over the siting of waste disposal and other noxious facilities (Lake 1987).

There has therefore been virtually no comparative research on participation in urban planning. Furthermore, most of the research on urban development politics has been carried out in the USA, and this debate has hitherto had a somewhat limited feel. The main objective of this report is to fill these gaps. Given the variations in political and local government systems, and alternative approaches to urban planning, we can expect the local politics of urban development to vary between countries. By comparing urban development politics in three contrasting European countries, we aim to broaden our understanding of participation in the planning process. In doing so, we will explore the implications of different forms of planning for participation and consider their policy implications for the UK.

A comparative case-study approach was adopted in this research. This helps to separate what is unique, in terms of explanatory variables, from what is general. Britain, France and Sweden were chosen because they represent extremes in formal and informal systems of government, urban planning and day-to-day development control.

In Chapter 1, we assess past research on forms of, and immediate influences on, planning participation in the UK. We also discuss the debate on urban-development politics as a variant of the literature on participation. In order to understand differences in participation between countries, it is necessary to consider its broader structural influences. We therefore also examine, in Chapter 1, the relationship between alternative forms of political organisation, the 'decision rules' governing urban planning and forms of participation.

Chapter 2 turns to the differences in political structures, and urban planning and local government systems in the three countries selected for analysis – Britain, France and Sweden. We consider *how* these might influence urban-development politics. In particular, we examine the various approaches to planning and development control and argue that these are likely to play an important part in shaping when and how public participation occurs. We also consider the implications of different degrees of autonomy in local government finance for the position taken by local authorities towards urban growth.

By focusing on specific growth regions in Britain, France and Sweden we then, in Chapters 3 and 4, examine the differences between urban-development politics and public participation in these countries. Chapter 3 examines formal and informal participation in the plan-formation process, while Chapter 4 discusses participation in decisions over specific development proposals.

Finally, in Chapter 5, we draw some conclusions. First, we consider the reasons for the differences in development politics in these countries. This returns us to the discussion in Chapters 1 and 2 on alternative approaches to urban planning and local government financial autonomy. Second, we consider the implications of the research findings for policy on planning participation in Britain.

Notes

1. Planning Policy Guidance Note No. 12 and the associated guide to good practice. See also sections 11 and 30 of the Town and Country Planning Act 1990.
2. *Planning: Charter Standards.* DOE, Welsh Office & National Planning Forum (1994); *Development Control. A Charter Guide.* DOE, Welsh Office & National Planning Forum (1993).
3. Quoted in *County News,* 1 May 1994, p.24.
4. Para. 3.2, *The Planning Inspectorate Executive Agency Business Plan 1993/94.* Bristol, DOE/Welsh Office (1993).
5. For example, Department of the Environment, *Publicity and Public Participation,* HMSO 1971.
6. Quoted in *The Builder,* 1989.
7. The DOE commissioned research on participation in the planning process; cf. Wilcox (1994a) on techniques for participation.

Acknowledgements

This book is based on a study funded by the Economic and Social Research Council (ESRC) (grant number R000232698). The initial impetus for the research was provided by two projects on housing provision in European growth regions and on housing and labour market interaction in Berkshire and the 'E4 Corridor' north of Stockholm. We are very grateful to ESRC for providing the funding for this research.

The research was started at the Centre for Urban and Regional Research, University of Sussex, and finished at the Policy Studies Institute, and I am grateful to both institutions for their support. I would also like to thank Simon Duncan, Peter Ambrose and Tim Edmundson for their help and advice. Kate Williams was responsible for many of the interviews in Berkshire. Margareta Dahlström provided invaluable help in setting up Swedish interviews and providing background information. Finally, I would like to thank all interviewees in the case-study areas for their time and help.

1 Participation, urban politics and forms of government

There are two distinct literatures from which we can draw the tools for understanding participation in the planning process. These focus on public participation – largely via the formation of community interest groups, but also groups with a specific interest in urban development – and secondly on the politics of urban development.

We argue that both these approaches have their limitations and in order to understand the differences in participation between countries, it is important to consider the relationship between structures of government and the dominant 'rules' within which planning decision-making takes place.

Planning participation and interest groups

'Participation' in planning can take many different forms, depending on the issues, the methods used, the point in the planning process at which it occurs, and the type of interests involved (Alterman 1982; Alterman et al 1984).

Some commentators have distinguished between 'top-down' forms of participation, initiated by planners or decision-makers, and 'bottom-up' forms, instigated by interest groups (Langton 1978). However, there are two important relationships involved in public participation in the planning process: the control exerted by planners in eliciting a response from the public and the response of the public to the planner (Alterman et al 1984).

Planners can influence participation in several ways. Clearly the types of technique used to elicit participation and the types of participant from which involvement is sought will play a part. Particularly important, however, is the stage in the planning process that the public becomes involved. Alterman et al (1984), focusing on the county structure plan process, felt that the limited effectiveness of participation reflected the late stage in plan preparation in which participation was usually undertaken. Because planners were seeking a reaction to a completed draft plan, their views were by this stage so crystallised they were hard to change. Alterman et al also concluded that contrary to popular belief, the low level of effective participation was not caused by the generality of structure plans, and a participant's immediate sphere interest did not necessarily limit his/her ability to make relevant responses to unrelated aspects of a plan.

Although local authorities usually lack formal or explicit policies towards liaison with groups, participation is often viewed by planners as a way of reducing the likelihood of objections to individual planning applications (Smith et al 1986). Planning authorities tend to regard close collaboration with groups as an important political resource for establishing good public relations for official policy. Nevertheless, in the past, participation has often simply meant keeping groups informed – Smith et al note that it is not surprising spontaneous action, rather than formal public participation, was a major feature of the 1980s. Where changes to plans took place, it was usually the result of the local authority's reaction to public pressure, rather than public involvement in the formative stages of a plan.

Participation can involve the formation of residents' or community groups. The crucial factor influencing the formation of such groups is generally held to be the presence of an external threat (or perceived threat) to existing local conditions. Most research suggests that it is the visibility of proposed development which causes a significant response by the public (for example, Simmie 1981). It has often been argued that many interest groups only become involved when they believe their interests are affected (Boaden et al 1980; RTPI 1982).[1]

Of course, certain sections of the public are more willing and able to become involved than others – the degree of involvement varies according to a wide range of factors such as socio-ecnomic position, education, language ability, confidence and mobility.

There are also differences in the nature of community groups. Smith et al (1986) identify two main forms:

- interest or sectional groups. These tend to be well-established and socially homogenous, frequently defending the status quo position in policy making. They consult with the local administration;

- promotional or cause groups. These are socially heterogeneous and advocate policy change. This type of group is more involved with the political arm of local government.

As well as residents seeking to defend their own interests, whether as part of a community group or as individuals, two further types of interest group can be distinguished (Boaden et al 1980). 'Major elites' are groups or individuals without whose cooperation or advice the local authority will find it difficult to adopt and implement plans. These might include elected representatives, public servants and external agencies. 'Minor elites' are voluntary organisations active in the area. These are frequently approached by local authorities in order to canvass the opinions held by a community.

Different types of issue generate varying degrees of participation. According to Alterman (1982) the extent of participation is likely to be influenced by such considerations as:

- the extent to which the issue involves conflicting interests;

- whether technical knowledge is required to understand the implications of a plan;

- the tangibility and immediacy of the plan's impact on potential participants; and

- its time perspective and degree of certainty.

Following on from this, much of the research on nimbyism has tended towards the view that the 'commodified' nature of residential land is a powerful influence on the social interests of homeowners. Locational conflicts can often be expressed as a defensive reaction by homeowners (e.g. Agnew 1981; Walker 1981; Pratt 1989). This further suggests that nimby-type action will be especially noticeable towards the end of periods of sustained economic expansion, since new urban development may threaten house prices. Some authors (Gleeson and Memon 1994; Dear 1992) have argued that the composition of nimby groups may be seen as a function of the type of externalities generated by the subject of the dispute, the types of land user in the vicinity of the scheme and their differing economic and social interests. It is generally held that better-educated, higher socio-economic status, older, settled individuals are more likely to become involved in exercises in participation (Hampton and Walker 1978).

Although the literature on planning participation touches on the degree to which property-related interests – in the form of homeowners – attempt to modify planning policy or development-control decisions, its focus tends to be on residents and their interest groups rather than other interests such as employers. Another problem with this research is that it has not been concerned with explaining international differences in participation – to what extent do alternative planning systems result in differences in the way participation occurs? To understand the wider politics of urban development – including the variety of ways in which groups with an interest in development interact – it is necessary to turn to the research on 'growth coalitions' and 'urban regimes'.

The politics of urban development – 'growth coalitions' and 'urban regimes'

In the 1980s there was growing interest in the formation of 'urban growth coalitions' embracing local government and the business community. 'Participation' in this model involves the promotion of urban development by business elites, with spin-off implications for anti-development activity.

The main thrust of the argument of Logan and Molotch[2], two of the main proponents of the concept, is that local elites with property interests coalesce into coalitions in order to persuade local government to provide better physical and social infrastructure. In this way, the demand for land and its value are increased. This process frequently brings about anti-development protest by local residents, largely because, unlike its costs, the benefits of growth are frequently only felt outside the locality. The fact that all residents are potential victims of development produces, according to Molotch and Logan (1984: 486), 'the potential for cross class coalition within the locality'.

This concept of growth coalitions has been criticised on a number of fronts (Lloyd and Newlands 1988; Cox and Mair 1989; Cox 1991a and b; Harding 1991. See Barlow 1995 for a summary). In particular, the assumption that land-based interests are a primary factor behind the formation of pro-growth coalitions is regarded as too simplistic (Cox and Mair 1989; Cox 1991a; Lloyd and Newlands 1988; Fainstein 1991).

Another problem is the lack of attention paid to anti-development politics. Despite the implicit part played in growth coalitions by local residents' or community groups, the focus is firmly on pro-growth politics. There has been some discussion about the role of particular values, often non-monetary, in promoting collective action over urban development (Molotch and Logan 1984, Cox 1991a). However, while such values are likely to be a cause of neighbourhood activism, this does not explain when and why common interests are transformed into popular uprisings (Fainstein 1991). The focus of research on growth coalitions tends to be the reasons for the privileged position of business in urban-development politics, rather than the reasons why, and ways in which, people protest about urban-development decisions.

A refinement of the growth coalitions concept focuses on 'urban regimes'. The concern here is essentially with the management of interests rather than their origin (Stone 1989; Stone et al 1991). This idea is potentially useful as an explanation for the interaction of different interest groups and local government in urban-planning issues. The emphasis here is on urban 'regimes' as a set of informal arrangements surrounding and complementing local government. Unlike the growth coalitions model, the concept of urban regimes does not simply concentrate on which groups have an interest in, and benefit from, growth. One of the proponents, Stone (1989), argues that shared opportunities for benefiting from growth are, in themselves, not specific and compelling enough to account for the effectiveness and durability of an urban regime. Policies which provide particular material incentives and benefits stand a better chance of reinforcing cooperation within a locality's governing coalition and are therefore more likely to endure. For its members an urban regime is therefore a means of achieving a coordinated effort which might not otherwise have been possible. Regimes are a mechanism for managing conflict and making adaptive responses to social change. This emphasis on cooperation means that the relationship between a regime's actors is its crucial distinguishing characteristic: who are the actors and how is cooperation achieved?

There are problems with the research on growth coalitions and urban regimes. In particular, its limited attention to the importance of the local context makes it hard to explain why different types of development politics arise at different times and in different places. Various explanations for the emergence of growth coalitions have been put forward, especially the degree of immobility or local dependence of firms (Cox 1991a) – more 'footloose' businesses are less likely to have an interest in promoting local growth. This notion has been subject to attack for its economic determinism (Fainstein 1991) and for overstating the difference in interests between local businesses and local branches of 'national' firms (Lloyd and Newlands 1988).

Another factor behind local differences in the forms of urban-development politics may be the extent of local government financial autonomy. Local authorities are faced with a potential contradiction between raising revenue through taxation, public expenditure on necessary social and physical infrastructure, and securing votes (Piven and Friedland 1984). This has implications for urban-development politics – it is possible that local authorities in government systems which place restrictions on their ability to raise finance locally and tightly control their public expenditure may be more concerned about 'costs' of urban development. These local authorities may face pressure on infrastructure provision if they are experiencing extensive urban development, yet only possess limited opportunities to pay for it. This may dampen 'pro-growth' attitudes in such authorities, leading to a tighter planning and development-control regime.

The fragmented nature of most studies – which focus on examples in a single country (for example, Lloyd and Newlands 1988; Vicari and Molotch 1990; Harding 1991; Keil and Lieser 1992) – means it is hard to draw conclusions about the conditions under which different forms of growth coalition or urban regimes emerge. According to Stone (1989), urban regimes can represent a useful means of promoting cooperation where local government is fragmented or the means for achieving formal coordination is poorly developed. And it is plausible that differences in systems of local government finance play a part in differences in growth politics. However, whatever the factors behind the emergence of an urban growth coalition or regime, these have to exist within a set of constraints imposed by the prevailing system of formal government control and the nature of the resources mobilised by participants in that system. To understand the differences in urban development politics, including the nature of participation, it is therefore necessary to develop an adequate understanding of the broad structural features of government and the rules within which planning decision-making occurs.

Government structures and the 'decision rules' of planning
Planning practice has often been described as the mediation of different identifiable interests within a set of rules and strategies (for example, Healey et al 1988). The process of policy formulation in urban planning involves the transformation of political pressures, ideas and problems into policies and policy measures. By identifying the potential political and administrative benefits, the criteria influencing who is involved in policy processes, the relations between those involved and the judgement as to what is an acceptable decision, Healey (1990) relates different forms of policy process to the decision rules they are governed by. In this way she differentiates between eleven forms of policy process. These are shown in Table 1 (see page 8) and range from more directly political forms, such as those involving clientelist relationships, through those involving a direct relation to interest groups – such as corporatism – to forms which are ostensibly separate from formal and informal politics and involve an indirect relation with interest groups ('techno-rational' or 'market-rational' forms).

Healey (1990) suggests that because interest groups are potentially excluded from policy decision-making, they have sought to wrest control of policy processes. This is achieved by either attempting to enter the policy-making process (by ensuring that procedures allow them a privileged position or negotiating over particular proposals) or by bargaining. Under the former, 'corporatist', approach, formalised negotiation between state agencies and specified powerful interests takes place. Examples in planning include the formerly privileged position of the Ministry of Agriculture, Forestry and Fisheries, or the way in which minerals operators and the housebuilding industry is consulted in structure planning.

There are some analogies between this view of interest groups' relations with the policy-making process and Rhodes and Marsh's work on political networks (see Rhodes 1986; Rhodes and Marsh 1992a, b). This suggests there is a range of different types of network, on a continuum from highly integrated 'policy communities' to loosely integrated 'issue networks'. These networks can be characterised by such features as differences in the level of membership, the frequency and quality of interaction between members, the degree of consensus over core issues, and the distribution of power resources. A policy community comprises a limited number of participants who interact frequently on all matters related to the policy issues. There is also a degree of constancy in its membership and values, the distribution of resources within the network is equal and the basic relationship between participants is one of exchange. There is therefore a balance of power between members of a policy community and, although one group may dominate, in the long run its survival requires that a balance of power between members is maintained.

The second method by which interest groups seek to become involved in policy-making is by bargaining (Healey 1990). This often involves a constant shift in concern from bargaining over specific sites to bargaining over policy and back again. Unlike the corporatist model, there are no formalised arenas or procedures. Its key feature is the fact that groups do not have common objectives, but recognise their mutual dependence. This exerts pressure on groups to arrive at an 'agreed' decision.

The analogy to this model under Marsh and Rhodes's schema is the 'issue network'. This comprises a large number of members, with a wide range of affected interests. Interaction between participants is likely to fluctuate in both frequency and intensity and, although a degree of agreement exists on basic values, conflict is also present. The unequal distribution of resources means that the basic type of relationship between participants is consultative, rather than one based on exchange. The inequalities in resources mean that power is unequally distributed within the network and a 'zero-sum' game prevails.

Healey (1990) points out that both corporatist and bargaining approaches to public involvement in policy-making are deliberately exclusionary in terms of public participation. Negotiation is usually only between selected interests. There are several ways of overcoming this. Public interest groups have pressed for tighter political control over planning bureaucracies to ensure officials implement plans as politically agreed. Alternatively, there have been attempts to remove the policy

Table 1 Process forms and decision rules

Process form	Potential/ political/ administrative	Criteria as to who is involved/ on what terms	Criteria as to the relations between those	Criteria as to what constitutes a good decision
CLIENTELIST	Direct political support	Individuals with specific demands; in return for specific or general support	Patron-client dependency; populist politics	Maintenance of dependency relations
POLITICO-RATIONAL	Direct political	Politicians; politically-selected policy analysts; conformity with political ideology	Conformity with party ideology and politics	Conformity with politi cal ideology
PLURALIST POLITICS	Legitimacy of state action determined competitively	Politically-active groups	Competition between position	Agreement of all parties and/or fair competition between participants
OPEN DEMOCRATIC	Legitimacy and effectiveness of state action	Politically-determined – via political ideology and voice; terms of entry negotiated	Open debate – fair hearing; discursive and/or oppositional resolution by vote	Informed by know-ledge and values of those affected by an issue
BARGAINING	Efficiency and effectiveness of state action	Mutually dependent parties in occasional rela-tion; involved to resolve a blockage, to allow each other to proceed	Negotiation around individual positions	Agreement of all parties
SPECIAL COMMITTEES	Legitimacy and effectiveness of state action	Expert etc personnel selected politically/ administratively; agenda limited but open within these limits	Discursive debating mode	Informed by specialist know-ledge and values
CORPORATIST	Efficiency and effectiveness of state action	Mutually dependent parties in continued relation; to maintain dominance by excluding other interests	Negotiation around a stream of present and future positions	Agreement of all parties and mainte-nance of continued working relations among those involved
BUREAU-CRATIC/ LEGAL	Legitimacy of state action	Legally/administratively defined interests; administrative process	Correct use of formal procedures	Correct use of pre-determined rules
JUDICIAL/ SEMI-DICIAL	Legitimacy of state action	Legally/administratively defined interests, around a legally/administratively filtered agenda of issues	Open debate, in investigative/ adversarial form	Fairness, reasonable-ness in UK; confor-mity with legal rules elsewhere in Europe?
TECHNO-RATIONAL	Legitimacy and effectiveness of state action	Technical experts define issues and interests, using expert knowledge and values	Scientific rationale of the issue in hand	Ends and means are related in a systematic way, informed by available knowledge
MARKET-RATIONAL	Efficiency of state action	Those with direct functional role	Functional rationale of the issues in hand	Efficiency – maximi-sing return on invest-ment, or minimum input/output costs

Source: Healey (1990: Table 2)

process from all those who have a stake in perpetuating particular kinds of institutional framework. This includes the use of expert committees, semi-judicial public inquiries and the development of forms of public debate. However, as Healey (1990) argues, all these assume policy ends and means can be articulated and evaluated, and conflicts can be resolved by discussion. A 'techno-rational' approach (see Table 1), whereby interests are distanced from the operation of state agencies by use of decision-making processes controlled by experts, was used in Britain in the 1960s to resolve major regional land allocation disputes. However, this fell into disuse partly because of politicians' fears they would lose control of policy ends to experts. A problem with semi-judicial processes involving an independent planning inspector is that they may readily be taken over by pressure groups representing different interests.

Conclusions

This chapter has argued that the literature on planning participation does not attempt to explain the differences in participation between countries or planning systems. In order to understand the reasons for any differences it is necessary to consider the various ways in which interest groups coalesce to promote or discourage urban development. There is now an extensive literature on urban-growth coalitions and urban regimes. However, while this sheds light on some of the possible reasons for local or national differences in urban-development politics, it can only take us so far. The growth coalitions model largely focuses on pro-growth, business-dominated movements, although it alludes to anti-development protest by residents. The concept of urban regimes provides a better model for understanding the management of interests involved in urban development, with its emphasis on the way policies are adopted to share out the benefits of growth. However, neither approach can explain why different types of development politics emerge at different times and in different places. The degree to which local business is 'immobile' may provide one explanation, as does the degree of local government autonomy.

These conclusions suggest that it is necessary to step back and examine the broad structural features of government and their implications for planning policy-making. This was the second task of this chapter. We argued that the way in which a government system operates – the degree of cooperation between government and interest groups, the extent to which levels of decision-making are fragmented – is likely to influence the rules by which planning policy is formulated. This in turn influences the nature of public participation in planning.

Our task in Chapter 2 is to examine the details of planning and local government systems in three contrasting European countries, before presenting our findings on participation in specific case-study areas.

Notes

1   See Cohen (1985), Ball and Millard (1986), Coxall (1986) for more detailed theories of motives for public involvement; Lowe (1986) for a critique of 'social bases' in the mobilisation process.

2   The concept of urban growth coalitions originated in the 1970s in the USA. See Stone (1976), Logan (1978), Molotch (1979), Friedland (1983), Molotch and Logan (1984, 1985), Logan and Molotch (1987), Molotch and Vicari (1987), Peterson (1987).

2 Government structures and urban planning

Chapter 2 examines the details of urban planning and government systems in Britain, France and Sweden. We first consider some of the broad features of European planning systems, before focusing on the three countries. Finally, we draw conclusions on the possible patterns of participation under the alternative approaches to planning and government.

European approaches to urban planning

There are three aspects to the control of urban development (Healey and Williams 1993):

- plan-making – outlining the strategies for organising land use;

- development – including land assembly and servicing, infrastructure provision and construction;

- regulation of building and redevelopment form and location.

There are, however, major differences in European planning systems in terms of these features. Broadly, we can distinguish between a continental European approach to land-use planning, whereby development plans are frequently accorded a legally-binding status, and the British approach, where plans merely have an advisory status. This is not to say that legally-binding plans automatically provide a framework which governs all the principles and rules of urban development. In some countries informal political networks operate and the actual pattern of urban development may diverge significantly from the objectives of the plan. In other cases, flexibility is introduced into the system by allowing 'fast-tracked' variations to plans or by letting plans lapse (see Healey and Williams 1993; GMA et al 1993).

There are also important differences in the development promotion function of urban planning, especially in terms of the role played by the public sector in supplying land for development. In most countries forms of private-public partnership emerged during the 1980s, in which local authorities or other public bodies were given responsibility for 'enabling' privately-initiated development. In some cases, though, the public sector plays a major role in assembling, servicing and supplying land for development. As Healey and Williams (1993) note, these differences have important implications for the capacity of authorities to coordinate different development activities and match these with plan priorities.

The third key area of planning is development control. Here, we can again identify a major difference between the British and continental European approaches. In Britain, development control is an administrative act, whereby decisions are taken by local politicians who are advised by planning officials. The decision is made on the basis of the matters contained in the local development plan, together with other material considerations. There is, therefore, a degree of discretion available to the local authority in granting the planning consent. In most other countries, however, land-use zoning is the norm. Under this approach, zoning plans and ordinances give property owners rights to develop their land according to the norms specified in the plan.

Britain, France and Sweden represent three contrasting approaches to planning and development control (see Barlow 1993; Barlow and Duncan 1994). The way in which local planning decision-making takes place and the approach towards public participation varies because of these differences.

In all three countries the formation of urban-development plans requires public participation, although this varies with the type of plan. Local land-use plans exist within a wider county or *département* strategic plans. These are known as structure plans in Britain, *översiktsplan* in Sweden and *schéma directeur d'aménagement urbain* (SDAU) in France.

United Kingdom

A British structure plan is significant because it frames the future distribution of new development between local authorities.[1] Structure plans are subject to public scrutiny, although since 1980 consultation does not involve matters for inclusion in the plan. Anybody who has made a formal objection to a structure or local plan has the right to be heard by an independent planning inspector at a public local inquiry.

Local authorities are obliged to draw up local plans detailing the desired location of various types of development and the likely future requirement for building land. These are also subject to public scrutiny. While these plans are an important consideration in judging development applications, they do not guarantee developers any right to build. Following the Town and Country Planning Act 1990, the planning system has arguably been strengthened, inasmuch that decisions must now be made in accordance with the local plan, unless material considerations indicate otherwise.

As we have noted, there is a requirement for publicity (rather than 'consultation') during the preparation of local plans and county-wide structure plans. This takes the form of a formal public inquiry, in which promoters of, and objectors to, a plan argue their cases. Challenges to the content of a plan can be made in the courts, but only on points of law. An authority will engage in public consultation when deciding on an application, but there are no third-party rights of protest for those with an indirect interest in the proposed development. There is also great variation in the practices of different local authorities, with some providing only the statutory minimum level of publicity for plans and others conducting major consultation exercises.

The granting of development consent is relatively discretionary, since the content of the local plan is only one factor in the local authority's deliberations. Local politicians play a significant role in sanctioning development, although political decisions on planning and development- control issues are taken in the light of advice from planning officers. In some areas it has been suggested that planners have increasingly become the 'servants' rather than guides of planning committees (Cheshire et al 1992).

Healey (1990) argues that the current British planning system is systematically biased in favour of certain interests. Bargaining is pervasive and developer interests are substantially privileged. Nevertheless, planning practice cannot be described as 'corporatist', nor can the 'decision rules' which govern the system can be seen as unchanging over time. The practices adopted in any given situation will be shaped by the way decision rules have evolved within the legacy of past forms. Several of the models described by Healey (1990) (see Chapter 1) have been used in Britain. For example, a 'techno-rational' approach, with experts defining the issues and interests, became popular in the 1960s and 1970s for the allocation of development land in structure plans, but subsequently fell into disuse. Special committees are also used for certain types of planning, especially urban conservation.

The normal approach, however, has been the use of semi-judicial processes, involving public inquiry, although in the 1980s there were moves towards a more market-led approach. According to Thornley (1991) there was a growing 'authoritarian decentralism', in which central government pushed planning decision-making ever-lower down the local government scale while maintaining firm ultimate control over planning decisions. Similarly anti-bureaucratic sentiments reduced 'official' local power and diminished the status of the planning profession (Coxall 1986). Today, the planning framework can arguably be said to have shifted back towards a more 'normal' semi-judicial approach, although elements of market-rationality remain – the Planning and Compensation Act 1991 re-emphasised the use of Simplified Planning Zones by local authorities, in which public participation and local inquiries are optional (Cameron-Blackhall 1994).

France

There are two levels of local planning in France (Booth 1989; Punter 1989; GMA et al 1993). *Schémas directeurs d'aménagement urbain* (SDAU) are broadly equivalent to British structure plans and set out long-term development policy for a *département* (county) as a whole. An SDAU has no legal standing and merely represents a set of broad development intentions. Public involvement in plan formation therefore tends to be limited. *Départements* are under no obligation to consult the public in discussions prior to a SDAU and relatively few communes or commune associations[2] publicise the particular proposals for their own locality. Certain bodies, such as chambers of commerce, are allowed to comment on specified issues, but in general any public comment has to be made through representation to local politicians. The consultation process for an SDAU is therefore frequently perceived to be a fairly feeble exercise, with discussions dominated by *département* and regional politicians and planning officers.

The second level – and the key plan for French communes – comprises the local land use plan (*plan d'occupation du sol* or POS). This establishes the nature, extent and location of future development. Local authorities *(communes)* with a population of over 10,000 are legally required to produce POS, but many smaller communes have adopted them voluntarily. A POS must be in accordance with an SDAU, where one exists; if there is no SDAU its legality must be checked by the *préfet* of the region. All POS must be approved by the local *préfet* and be consistent with the national framework of town planning laws and regulations. These plans are subject to public consultation, although communes revising a POS are only obliged to present their proposals at a meeting with residents' groups before the start of the public inquiry. Proposals in a POS can, however, be challenged in the courts *(tribunal administratif)*. The key factor determining whether a plan, or amendments to it, is deemed illegal is conformity with an existing SDAU.

The system of land-use zoning means that detailed local plans essentially comprise a legally-binding document containing the right to develop. Large areas of the countryside (as well as urban areas) are left unzoned and in these cases the national development norms apply. Because of the zoning systems, the process of obtaining development consent is potentially straightforward. A building permit is needed for all forms of development and is granted according to a written timetable, with the responsibility resting with the mayor of the commune.

Local politicians are therefore important in French planning and development control – perhaps even more so than in Britain. The very small size of communes, together with the extensive power of their mayors, means there is potentially a closer relationship between individual politicians and planning decision-making. There is also a degree of osmosis between institutions and officials of central and local government. This arises from the *cumul des mandats,* whereby local politicians accumulate political offices in different tiers of government[3] (Ashford 1983; Mény 1983; Keating 1991). This potentially blurs the distinction between those who sanction development and those to whom the public can protest. However, although mayors are in principle free to act, their decisions are subject to scrutiny by the *préfet.* Mayors are generally involved in a web of relations at a supra-communal level (Booth 1993). These include the technical planning officers of the *département* and, in some cases, the officers of the local *agence d'urbanisme.* The latter have been established in major metropolitan areas in order to coordinate planning and provide technical backup for the conurbation as a whole.

Although local conditions vary because of the part played by local mayors, development consent is rarely refused, provided the proposed scheme is in accordance with the POS or the national development norms. There is, however, an appeal system for third parties to protest about planning decisions through the administrative courts.

The French system of planning and development control can perhaps be described as one which is dominated by a bureaucratic-legal approach (see Chapter 1). Local plans are legally binding once adopted and decisions are taken on the basis of their correspondence with pre-determined rules. The planning system also contains elements of market-rationality and corporatism. In France – as in Britain and elsewhere – the 1980s saw a growing concern over the need to regenerate older urban environments and transform the specific qualities of different localities so that they could better support local firms and attract new investment. This meant that land-use planning became increasingly tied to local economic development strategies, and one result was the introduction of more corporatist forms of urban planning in some urban areas. From the mid-1970s to 1984, a *Programme d'Action Foncière* had enabled French communes in major conurbations to use low-interest loans to buy land for their future development needs. However, this pro-active role by local authorities was increasingly replaced in the 1980s by the use of public-private partnerships, with the public sector reduced to a largely 'enabling' role. In areas being brought forward for development, the POS is now often replaced by a 'concerted development zone' *(zone d'aménagement concerté* or ZAC) (Punter 1989). Some of the development on this type of land is carried out by public-private partnerships between local authority and developer *(société d'économie mixte*, SEM).[4]

Sweden

Sweden stands in stark contrast to both Britain and France. Here, there is a markedly interventionist approach to urban planning. As well as having the power to establish public land banks for housing development, communes formulate five-year housing development plans. As in France, a Swedish local structure plan *(översiktsplan)* has no legal standing and essentially represents a set of development intentions. An *översiktsplan* lasts for a comparatively long period – typically 20 years – although it can be modified during this time. It is not seen as the definitive planning document for a commune. The plan is subject to a public consultation exercise. As with British structure plans, this takes place in two phases. Greater emphasis is given to consultation on the first draft of the plan, so that any problems can be ironed out before a revised draft of the plan is presented to the public.

The key plan for Swedish communes is the local land-use plan *(detaljplan)*, together with guidance from the regional authority. This is essentially a zoning plan which establishes the nature, extent and location of future development. These plans are subject to public consultation and can be challenged in the courts; consequently they tend to attract more public attention. Since the 1987 Planning and Building Act Swedish communes have been obliged to consult *all* residents affected by a *detaljplan,* and not simply landowners. In addition, any registered community group, together with other registered organisations such as employers' federations, public housing companies and major local employers, is automatically consulted about detailed proposals. Community and other interest groups can ask to be placed on the commune's list of official consultees.

Development control therefore involves zoning with legal rights, with potential development land released from the public land banks according to the requirements of local plans (Barlow 1993). Zoning of land for development implies the right for the communes to take this land into public ownership. The Swedish system also embodies a third-party right of protest.

To some extent the policy process and decision rules of the Swedish planning system can be described as involving open debate and bargaining, using the typology of Table 1 (see page 8). There are signs, however, that this consensus approach is slowly breaking down in urban planning. Since 1987 communes must communicate their future planning intentions with all affected residents, but local plans no longer need the approval of County Administrative Boards. Some commentators have concluded that this may reduce local democratic input into the planning process with consultation becoming a token exercise (see Forsberg 1991). Furthermore, there has been a rift in the 'popular movements coalition' of the housing sector – comprising the National Association of Municipal Housing Companies (SABO), the National Federation of Tenants Associations *(Hyresgästernas Riksförbund)* and the Social Democratic Party – over the introduction of market principles (Elander and Strömberg 1992).

Conclusions

We argued in Chapter 1 that there is a relationship between the political framework within which planning decision-making takes place and the nature of participation in the planning process. We also noted that different types of political network are likely to exist, defined by their membership characteristics, degree of integration and focus. Of particular interest, to use the typology of Marsh and Rhodes (1992a and b), are 'issue networks', which bring together a large number of participants with a wide range of interests, and 'policy communities', in which there is a limited number of relatively equal participants. This chapter examined the political structures and contrasting approaches to urban planning in Europe, focusing on Britain, France and Sweden.

It has often been argued that issue groups emerge when formal political channels offer little scope for influencing government policy (for example, Lowe 1986). The findings of this chapter suggest that such a situation could arise under a variety of different political structures. Under the French model of 'bureaucratic planning', for example, the fact that the key political figure at a local level is the commune mayor, together with the *cumul des mandats,* may make formal political parties less likely to be a channel of popular protest. This possibility has been reinforced by the decentralisation reforms of the early 1980s which increased the powers of mayors without introducing greater rights of public participation in local decision-making processes (Goodchild et al 1993).

In Britain, a different model has also led to a central role for issue groups in planning protest. The partial adoption of a more market-rational approach to planning in the 1980s to some extent resulted in a downgrading of public participation, by increasingly removing decision-making from local authorities. Under this framework issue groups are said to have formed less visible relationships with the state, by bargaining, cultivating 'insider' contacts or entering local politics (Lowe 1986).

Under Swedish social-democratic corporatism a 'one-nation' version of the welfare state means that state allocation has replaced the market to much greater extent than in other capitalist countries. Here, a process of 'structured consultation' is said to potentially allow interest groups considerable opportunities to participate in decision-making (Castles 1978; Heclo and Madsen 1987). However, the political system has traditionally co-opted individual protest into a broader mobilisation at a supra-local scale. The principal players are the local controlling party (or parties), together with local commune officials and those (for example, housing co-operative managers) who have frequent involvement in commune deliberations. Debate therefore tends to be via political parties, unions and officially-sanctioned groups.

As well as affecting the formation and nature of protest groups, these differences in broad political structures may also shape the way involvement in urban planning by the business community occurs. The British business community is generally held to be highly fragmented and parochial at the local level. In addition, the delivery system for business services is fragmented and confused, with no effective integration between organisations and an uneven geographic spread. This has made the intervention in the planning process by many business interests hard, since most – excluding development-related interests – have been excluded from the policy process.

In contrast, the status of business organisations under public law in France and some other European countries ensures greater potential participation by the business community. The relative strength of French chambers of commerce is reinforced by compulsory membership and their ability to levy fees (Bennett et al 1993, 1994). Here, potentially at least, there are formal procedures for involvement in policy processes. In Sweden, in contrast, business-lobbying tends to take place through formal channels at a regional or national level and local chambers of commerce tend to be weaker.

There may also be a relationship between the type of planning and development-control system and the way in which participation occurs. The more discretionary British system may afford more opportunities for intervention, since this could occur when plans are established and when individual planning applications and decisions are made. A strict zoning system, on the other hand, suggests that intervention is likely to occur during the plan-making process, but opportunities for participation may be more limited once zoning has been established. Protest over specific development approvals may be muted or impossible, although this is dependent on the rights accorded to individuals under the legal system. Similarly, under the Swedish approach, public intervention will be most likely at the plan-making and zoning stage. However, there may be further intervention when a local authority is buying land for its land bank, and thus identifying future development sites.

Notes
1. The role of structure plans may be downgraded in the future.
2. The small size of communes has led to the provision of powers enabling them to form larger voluntary local government units for planning and infrastructure provision (see Appendix 1).
3. Up to five are allowed, including membership of the European Parliament.
4. Britain saw similar trends in the 1980s, with the introduction of a range of non-elected development agencies and a renewal of corporatist forms of representation (Shaw 1993). Healey and Williams (1993) argue that Britain represents an extreme position because the strong development role played by the public sector was replaced by a regulatory role which gave significant scope to the market as the principal driving force.

3 Public participation in plan formation

Chapters 1 and 2 discussed the broad 'decision rules' and government structures within which planning systems are situated, and the different approaches to urban planning in Britain, France and Sweden. We also looked at the implications for public participation. We now turn to the details of participation – its extent and nature – in the alternative planning systems. Chapter 3 discusses participation in plan formation and Chapter 4 discusses participation in development control.

Selecting the case-study regions

In order to investigate the differences in public participation in the three countries and separate what is unique, in terms of explanatory variables, from what is general, we adopted a comparative case-study approach. It was felt that such an approach would help untangle the dynamics of the relationship between the broad structural features of government, intra-national influences and forms of urban-development politics. Britain, France and Sweden represent extremes in formal and informal systems of government, urban planning and day-to-day development control. Areas within each country which have experienced a recent employment and population boom are likely to face more intense political pressures over the costs and benefits of growth. This might include pro-development lobbying by businesses, including developers and landowners, and 'nimbyism' by local residents. Case-study areas in the three countries (see below) which had been used in previous comparative research on the effectiveness of different forms of planning for housing provision were therefore chosen[1]. These comprised the central Berkshire segment of the 'M4 Corridor', the 'E4 Corridor' north of Stockholm, the southern suburbs of greater Paris, and the Toulouse metropolitan region (see Figure A1, page 70).

The case-study areas had originally been chosen to be as comparable as possible in analytical terms – they had similar employment structures and similar growth rates. In each, sustained and rapid employment growth and economic restructuring had taken place during the 1980s, both in absolute terms and in relation to national averages. The accent was on 'high-tech' manufacturing, financial and producer services, and research and development; each had comparatively high levels of well-paid professional, managerial and skilled technical employees. Appendix 1 provides a description of urban development and local government in these areas.

Formal and informal participation in the case-study areas

The patterns of participation in the case-study areas were remarkably similar in terms of the types of interest group involved and issues which generated the greatest controversy. Most formal responses to local plans concerned specific development proposals and were made by residents' or single-issue groups. Typical issues were the volume of traffic and loss of green space. There was comparatively little formal intervention by the business community, although developers and landowners tended to have a higher profile. In all the case-study areas there was some concern by the business community that the mechanisms for its inclusion in the consultation process were weak.

The main objection by interest groups in all the case-study areas was that consultation only took place once the parameters of the plan had been set. Plans were also regarded as insufficiently detailed, making it hard to determine their implications for a specific neighbourhood. Access to planning officers and local politicians was seen as variable; some interviewees felt that it was largely dependent on planners' and politicians' perceptions of the importance of particular issues and the need to consult the public.

The experience of public participation in the revisions to the Toulouse POS and the preparation of the SDAU for the Plateau de Saclay in South Paris illustrate the problems for would-be participants in the French planning process (see case studies 1 and 2). We will later see that groups in the British and Swedish case-study areas faced similar problems.

Lack of information about specific proposals and the limited opportunities for participation in planning policy decisions were highlighted as key problems by community groups in both the French case-study areas. These problems appear to be inherent in the French system, although their extent varies according to the nature of the local political and planning administration. Toulouse was seen as an especially problematic area by community groups. One pointed out that Montpelier, another city which saw extensive growth during the 1980s, was able to involve local residents in public inquiries in a more participatory way.

Case Study 1   Revising the Toulouse POS

Background
The growth of Toulouse has occurred in three distinct phases, each characterised by a different spatial form. From the late 1950s to the late 1960s large-scale development of suburban estates took place, mainly comprising social housing. The 1970s was also dominated by suburban expansion, this time largely of single-family housing for owner-occupiers *(pavillons)*. By the mid-1980s the Toulouse commune decided it was necessary to reduce the pressure of commuting and encourage the redevelopment of sites in the city centre. The city was also seeing extensive job and population growth. An influx of skilled workers was seen as highly beneficial to the city's economy and the commune felt it was important to reinforce the attractiveness of Toulouse by upgrading the housing stock. The revision of the city's POS in 1985 therefore aimed to encourage the development of new apartment housing in central Toulouse. There were several increases to the permitted plot ratios (the COS, *coefficient d'occupation du sol*).

The fourth revision of the POS
There was great concern over the 'intensification' of Toulouse under the 1985 POS. The plan led to a large increase in housebuilding in the city centre. In 1982 28 per cent of all housing completions in the agglomeration were in Toulouse commune. By 1988 this proportion had reached 70 per cent. In addition, there was a boom in hotel and office development.

The redevelopment of sites at higher densities spurred a well-organised and large protest movement. There was already an umbrella group for 35 neighbourhood residents' groups *(comités de quartiers)*, the *Union des Comités des Quartiers* (UCQ). This had originally been formed in 1979, with the objective of increasing participation in the planning process and providing planning advice to local residents groups. Another group – *Toulouse ProPOS* – was founded in 1989. This aimed, according to one representative, to tackle 'the causes of the problem, the POS, rather than the consequences' (that is, individual development decisions).

UCQ saw the increase in the COS as an insidious process which was leading to an incremental rise in densities. In areas where the COS was raised developers would inevitably build up to the maximum allowed. This eroded the amenity standards of neighbouring residents, especially through the loss of light and trees. In response to the protests of UCQ and other groups, the mayor of Toulouse said that these problems would be corrected by the fourth revision of the POS, beginning in 1989.

During the consultation for the fourth revision, UCQ and *Toulouse ProPOS* submitted a number of specific proposals to reduce commuting by car. The two organisations also questioned the basis for intensification, arguing that the commune had not justified its claims for new housing development. This, they argued, was borne out by the vacancy rates in housing, office and hotel schemes.

Other participants in the consultation process were also concerned about the effects of rapid growth – the main problem for the chamber of commerce was transport infrastructure. Nevertheless, both the chamber and the *Observatoire Immobilière* (a group providing housing market information for local developers and estate agents) were also in favour of redeveloping the *pavillon* zone surrounding the city centre. Both organisations were concerned about the 'restrictiveness' of the new POS, which was claimed to be one reason for the rise in house and land prices. At the public inquiry the inspector found UCQ's points 'interesting', but argued that a new inquiry would be needed if the proposals were to be taken on board.

Even though the UCQ and *Toulouse ProPOS* were unsuccessful in their attempts to modify the fourth POS, they nevertheless feel that they were successful in gaining public support. This meant the commune had to take more notice of the public for the fifth revision (beginning in 1993). The two groups were able to create a tripartite discussion between the commune's planners, developers and residents' associations (over 40 are involved). This has already had some success in influencing the commune, which has toned down some of its proposals for intensification in some areas. Nevertheless, the UCQ and *Toulouse ProPOS* still feel that the commune's position is that a reduction in development in one area has to be matched by an increase in another.

Variable access to planning officers and politicians, in a situation where local mayors wield considerable discretion as to how much consultation is allowed, was a particular problem. A mayor from one South Paris commune claimed to consult the local residents' group only when it suited him, and in any case there was no need for consultation since he had lived in the commune for 40 years and knew everybody! Another mayor (from the Toulouse area) claimed to have set up a special commission to consult the public but there had been no interest from local residents.

Although Toulouse's deputy mayor responsible for planning held a number of meetings with community groups, these maintained that information about the commune's plans was hard to obtain in advance and often inaccurate or out-of-date. Furthermore, most of the information about revisions to the POS was published in a local city newsletter, *Capitole-Information*. This is funded by contributions from local employers, and groups were therefore concerned that information was skewed to stress the merits of growth.

There was also anxiety about the amount of secrecy in the way decisions about the revisions to Toulouse's SDAU and POS were made. According to one group, essential decisions about the POS were made behind closed doors in the commissions dealing with the SDAU. The only public participants in these discussions were from the employers' federation. Decisions taken by SDAU commissions were then turned into concrete

Case Study 2   Plateau de Saclay

Background
The Plateau de Saclay is located 30 kms south of Paris and covers almost 5,000 hectares. The plateau includes 15 communes (10 in the département of Essonne and 5 in Yvelines), with a total population of 109,010 in 1990. Population growth in the 1980s was moderate, increasing by some 9,000, but the Plateau is located in the 'Axe-Sud', a major growth corridor south of Paris. It is estimated that approximately 40 per cent of France's research capability is on the Plateau itself or in the surrounding area and the regional government for Ile de France decided in the mid-1980s to reinforce this position by creating a 'technopole'. In 1987, the *Préfet* for Ile de France therefore directed the *Préfets* for Essonne and Yvelines to set up an inter-communal body to cooperate over the establishment of a SDAU for the Plateau. Accordingly, in December 1988 a *syndicat intercommunal* was established, bringing together the 15 communes (one commune subsequently withdrew). In January 1992 a *district intercommunal* was set up, providing a more binding form of contract between communes *(district intercommunal du Plateau de Saclay,* DIPS).

The SDAU proposals
The *départements* have asked that the SDAU achieves a balance between employment and housing growth. There are therefore plans for the construction of 2,900 dwellings on the Plateau and a further 10,000 in the surrounding communes. A non-legally binding *programme locale de l'habitat* (PLH) is being established for the plateau. This is an assessment of the extra housing needs arising from employment growth and a housing capacity study of each commune. The PLH is not intended to specify the location of the new housing and it is expected that communes will reserve land for residential development through their own POS. Under an agreement with the Ile de France region the SDAU also safeguards 2,000 ha. of farmland and open space.

Public participation and the DIPS planning process
Three main community groups are involved in the SDAU participation process: the *Association de la Défense de la Vallée de la Bièvre,* the *Amis de la Parc Régionale,* and *Yvelines Environnement.* There are links between these groups and other associations outside the Plateau area, in particular a group concerned with the development proposals in the nearby commune of Massy (see case study 10, page 42).

Representatives of environmental groups (via the *Union des Associations de Sauvegard du Plateau de Saclay)* were involved in the initial discussions about the formation of the *syndicat intercommunal.* However, they felt that central government had gone back on its word – originally given in the 1960s – to preserve the plateau for farmland and open space. The main concern of these groups therefore turned to the construction of new roads and the development of the plateau.

Commune mayors claimed that the decisions taken by the DIPS are initially discussed in the commune and then publicised. However, some mayors and planners clearly saw the community groups as a hindrance – as one mayor put it,

> As soon as you propose something an association is formed. Some are against all urban development ... they are too powerful and are only concerned with their own environment. They are not 'green' as a whole ... As soon as a decision is made by the DIPS it's attacked by associations. They just want to keep the Plateau green.

This respondent also felt that associations are good at publicity:

> They go to a *Tribunal Administratif* or the *Conseil Général* and claim 5,000 people are against a proposal. In reality 4,500 people won't have understood the issue.

Community groups felt that participation in the planning process was hard. One group said that it had found the DIPS very bad at communicating its proposals, although this was probably more a question of communication skills than secrecy. It accepted that communes hold open meetings, despite the fact that associations have no right to be consulted. It was suggested that under these circumstances it becomes essential to nurture 'personal relations' with mayors and planning officers.

It is clear there is public concern over the development proposals – this is evidenced by the 20 per cent share of the vote achieved by the Greens in the 1992 local elections. Tapping into this, the major environmental groups have had some success in stopping the A14 motorway proposals and delaying the construction of a new Renault R&D centre.

proposals by planning officers. The public only heard about these at the public inquiry, by which time the proposals were relatively fixed. Furthermore, public inquiries were felt to be poorly organised. It is perhaps noteworthy that the local chamber of commerce also believes the Toulouse POS is hard to challenge, with the power residing with the mayor.

A lack of information about proposals in plans – both SDAU and POS – appears to be an endemic feature of the French system. However, in the case of Toulouse there was the additional problem that the POS had been subdivided into 28 neighbourhood plans, delivered bit by bit. Community groups argued this made it hard for them to obtain a city-wide view of the proposals and potentially set one neighbourhood against another.

In South Paris the consultation about the SDAU for the Plateau de Saclay (case study 2, page 24) appears to have been conducted on a more open basis. However, although local environmental groups were involved in early decisions on the SDAU, there remained a feeling amongst these groups that participation was limited. This is partly because of the lack of communication from communes and the inter-communal association about specific proposals.

Case Study 3   Järfälla local plan

Background
Järfälla commune was subject to intense development pressure throughout the 1980s, and the 1990 structure plan aimed to increase local employment to reduce commuting. Several major employment sites were proposed, along with new housing developments. The latter are partly the result of the Stockholm Regional Authority's aims to redistribute housebuilding throughout the region.

Public participation in the 1990 Järfälla local plan
The consultation process for the 1990 Järfälla plan involved two main discussion phases. This dealt with the general objectives for the commune and detailed land-use plan. The first phase saw representations from 120 organisations or individuals on general features of the plan, and a further 250 comments on specific topics. The second phase involved 60 representations. Phase 1 began in the summer of 1988 and was complete by April 1990. Phase 2 was relatively short and the plan was accepted in November 1990.

Every proposal in the plan was discussed in detail with local politicians from each party. In addition, the commune holds quarterly meetings with all the neighbourhood groups and the local branch of the *Naturskyddsföreningen*. This is part of a national environmental pressure group. The Järfälla branch was established in 1967 and has 1,500 members, of which perhaps 200 are active. Membership has remained stable since 1990, although there was a sharp increase in the 1980s, during the period of growth pressure. This organisation felt that politicians listened more to residents' groups than other interest groups. Because of this, they had created a residents' group in one area, which had been more successful in attracting the attention of politicians. In general, the interviewees believed that smaller political parties were generally more approachable but had limited influence; there was no difference between the Social Democrats and Moderates, which were both 'pro-development'. The Centre Party was seen as too 'green' and not taken seriously by other parties, although the *Naturskyddsföreningen* believed its influence might grow given the new political balance of power following the 1991 elections.

Being a registered group seemed to provide better access to planning officials and politicians. One local residents' group said that until it was registered it 'had to go fishing' to discover the commune's future plans. Nevertheless, this group still felt that access to planners and politicians was variable, depending on the issue. It argued that if the right planner could be identified early enough in the planning process, it was easier to intervene successfully.

Broadly, the view of community and residents' groups was that while they were automatically consulted, it was also necessary to approach local politicians informally. Once a detailed land-use plan is established, it becomes hard to effect any changes, hence early intervention in the planning process was seen as essential. However, detailed information about proposals was not always forthcoming. As one interviewee put it, 'it is not always easy to intervene early enough – you have to be able to anticipate what is in the planners' minds'.

A further problem, according to one small residents' group (with only 15 members), was that there is usually not enough help to interpret more technical issues. This group had, however, invited local politicians and planners to advise on the implications of proposals for a new employment zone, and felt that this had allowed it to develop an adequate response.

As well as formal participation in the planning process, some use was made of informal meetings with planning officers and local politicians. Local groups occasionally met commune mayors but little use was made of other politicians. This may have been an effect of *cumul des mandats,* the multiple offices held by politicians (see Chapter 2). This was regarded as a major problem by some of the Toulouse community groups. The fact that the president of the *syndicat intercommunal* (intercommunal association) for the conurbation was also the mayor of Toulouse was felt to have resulted in a concentration of too much planning power in one individual's hands.

The Swedish system stands in stark contrast to that of France, despite the fact that interest groups expressed similar anxieties as their French counterparts about the nature of public participation. While the system had clear formal mechanisms for participation, informal intervention – approaching planners and politicians outside the recognised consultation period – was seen by many as essential. There was a general feeling that the 1987 Planning Act had not had much effect on the level or nature of participation, since it was merely a public declaration of existing practice. Local plan consultation exercises attracted a large number of formal participants. In one commune – Upplands Väsby – almost 400 groups or individuals made written comments; another commune – Järfälla – attracted 430 representations in its consultation exercise (see case study 3).

A local structure plan *(översiktsplan)* tends to attract less attention from local residents than the detailed land-use plan *(detaljplan)*. The feeling among planners was that most discussions about a structure plan were conducted between local officers and members, with only limited input by other organisations or the public. There was some concern amongst officials to speed up the consultation process for both plans as a whole, which could take well over two years.

Community and residents' groups, as well as businesses, argued that discussions early in the planning process were essential for successful participation. Groups therefore all regularly approached local politicians and planners. This was feasible for well-organised and officially-sanctioned interest groups, but other groups often felt excluded. Smaller political

---

Case Study 4   Public participation in Berkshire's structure plan

Two community groups are especially important in Berkshire. Sane Planning in the South East (SPISE) and the Northern Parishes Action Group (NORPAG). SPISE was formed in 1986 to fight the growth of planning by appeal and represents a collective community view at public planning inquiries and other public participation exercises. The group also aims to provide the public with education about planning issues. NORPAG has similar aims and also sees one of its most important roles as raising public awareness of planning issues. Both groups represent smaller organisations and encourage participation by the public.

NORPAG and SPISE have become increasingly professional in both their approach and organisation over the years. As SPISE's vice president commented '...the banners have given way to skilful lobbying of ministers and civil servants'. By becoming more professional SPISE has secured itself an important advisory position within the planning system. It meets the County Council regularly and is on the Department of the Environment's list of consultees for relevant papers. SPISE also acts as advisors to SERPLAN (the standing conference on regional planning matters).

Broadly, since the mid-1980s these groups have performed a role of 'planning watch-dogs', commenting on planning procedure, keeping the public informed of local issues, and lobbying at a national level. Both were in favour of concentrated discussion during the plan-formation stage, since this lessens the chance of ambiguity at appeals by clarifying planning intentions.

---

parties were generally regarded as more approachable, although one interviewee said that many politicians believed they already adequately represented the public, and regular consultation was therefore unnecessary. However, an important feature of the Swedish system is the frequency of elections[2] which means that if development proposals can be delayed by a year or so they frequently enter the electoral battleground. Strict proportional representation means that political control is easily lost – and gained – and single issues can thus become politically crucial.

Berkshire displayed similar features (see case study 4). Here, the formation of highly-organised interest groups in the mid 1980s was a response to the perceived lack of participation in the planning process (cf. Short et al 1986; Barlow and Savage 1986). Planners here commented that the scale of this involvement was a relatively recent phenomenon. Two groups had become increasingly professional in their organisation and approach, aiming to represent a collective community view. In doing so they had secured an important advisory position within the planning system. As well as regular meetings with the County Council and District Councils, they produced reports for regional planning conferences, carried out their own research and lobbied on a national level.

An important difference between Britain and the other countries is the role of the local press as a forum for public discussion. This is virtually non-existent in the E4 Corridor and South Paris, although Toulouse, as a major free-standing city, has its own local media. Many residents' groups and employers' federations felt that the lack of a local press stifled public discussion and reduced the flow of information from local authorities to the wider population. In parts of the E4 Corridor and South Paris, chambers of commerce and other employers had discussed the possibility of establishing local newspapers. In Berkshire, in contrast, the local media is stronger and acts as an important channel for information and discussion.

One aspect of planning participation in Berkshire is common in the E4 Corridor and South Paris. In these areas, development-related industry has ensured that its interests are considered at the earliest possible stages of plan formation. This was even the case in Sweden, where the highly publicly-directed development system might be expected to dampen the activities of landowners and developers. Developers and landowners, aware that concentrated lobbying at draft-plan stages could reap long term gain, tended to make considerable efforts to promote specific proposals. For example, HSB (the national social housing developer) had regular informal contact with all the leading local politicians and claimed that establishing a dialogue was crucial to the success of any development proposals. According to a local social housing company it had become easier to participate in the planning process since the 1987 Act. Before the Act it claimed that planners made their decisions and then went out to consultation. Under the old system the company met planners once a year and made formal written representations on the local housing and planning programme. Since 1987 the system had become more flexible and there was more informal contact on a face-to-face basis.

Weak mechanisms for local industry participation were a feature of all three planning systems. In Berkshire, for example, discussions with planners and chambers of commerce suggested that non-developer firms rarely intervened in the planning process. In the 1988 Berkshire structure plan most formal submissions were from landowners, developers and their agents. In all there were 61 such submissions, compared to 21 from other businesses. In contrast, formal participation by non-property related businesses was muted. Local business organisations such as the chambers of commerce, the Berkshire Business Group and retailers' associations all commented on the structure plan, especially on the need to improve infrastructure and transport provision. However, individual firms made only a small number of representations to the structure plan (21) and most responses were about company-specific issues.

Nevertheless, some major employers had not been reticent about making their views clear to planning authorities. For example, in April 1991 the company secretary of Hewlett-Packard spoke on behalf of several multinational companies at a conference to consider the future quality of life in the area, complaining (Thompson 1991: 2):

> our perception is that although there is a statutory consultation period there is no real effort to discover what industry actually wants.

On the other hand, the comments by the Berkshire Business Group – representing several large employers – on the structure plan were distinctly muted (RCB 1990: 17):

> ...while past growth rates have caused congestion and environmental problems and cannot continue indefinitely, it is imprudent at this stage for the Business Group to advocate either restraint or growth policies for different types of development.

This response is perhaps surprising, given that at the time there were severe housing-related recruitment difficulties (Barlow 1990), and a survey showed that 50 per cent of firms believed they would increase their workforce in the next three years and 51 per cent of those looking for new sites were doing so in Berkshire (RCB 1990). The explanation may lie in the fact that many businesses were more concerned to provide financial help with housing costs directly to their employees, rather than to lobby for more homes (Barlow 1990).

In part, the general lack of participation by non property-related industry can be explained by the business community's relative lack of organisation, at least in the cases of Berkshire, the E4 Corridor and South Paris. We argued in Chapter 2 that the British business community is locally fragmented and parochial, with an inadequate system for delivering business services. In contrast, in France, the status of business organisations under public law, compulsory membership of chambers of commerce and their ability to levy fees, means businesses are potentially better integrated into planning decision-making at the local level. However, in the French case-study areas the input by chambers of commerce and private firms was in fact restricted to comments on such issues as plot densities and car parking arrangements. Chambers complained their comments were limited by the official rules of participation.

In Sweden, it was argued in Chapter 2 that business-lobbying tends to take place through formal channels at a regional or national level. Nevertheless, there were signs that major employers were involved in local

---

Case Study 5   Business participation in Swedish local plans

In two E4 Corridor communes a major supermarket chain and a local retailers' organisation were unhappy because they claimed that in each commune the detailed land-use plan had not followed the strategic plan. The supermarket chain had discussed a new out-of-town scheme for over two years with politicians and planners and had bought the site after a receiving a favourable reaction. When the detailed plan was published the site zoned for retail use had been moved 200 metres because of public concern over traffic.

The retailers' organisation was dissatisfied because the lack of detailed information in the plan allowed planners and politicians the flexibility to change their original intentions. Although the commune had established a liaison officer to deal with the retailers' organisation and it met planners and politicians up to three times a year, it felt it was hard to find out what was being proposed. As an example, it cited the *översiktsplan* which had identified the need for only one local shopping centre and prevented its expansion; subsequently the chief planner and the Director of the Commune produced a plan for a 5,000m^2 district centre, less that 1 km from the existing centre.

In Upplands Väsby the main problem faced by the commune was to secure a better balance between job growth and housing provision, thereby reducing commuting flows. Although there was broad consensus amongst politicians about the annual housebuilding requirement, there were differences of opinion about the tenure and type of housing, and the specific location of new development. Some firms had experienced housing-related labour shortages during the boom years of the 1980s – Marabou, the largest local employer, saw an annual labour turnover of 42 per cent in 1990 and was obliged to bus workers from Enköping (some 80 kms away). This firm submitted to the local strategic plan inquiry that its employees should have priority in the housing waiting list and expressed concern that housebuilding had declined. On the other hand, the local employers' federation (Väsby Företagen) argued that the housing exchange (waiting list) could be made to work more efficiently. This organisation also wished to see a higher rate of housebuilding and a better mix of housing tenures.

---

lobbying over planning matters. Several commune planners in the E4 Corridor felt that large companies were increasingly lobbying local politicians (case study 5). Firms would intervene to promote their own future plans or short-circuit the commune's housing waiting list on behalf of their employees. In some cases, 'planning gain' – community benefits – had been offered to communes by firms as an incentive. However, this lobbying was uncoordinated. Individual firms tended to negotiate directly with planners and local politicians. One major employer said they met the local council and planning officers once a year to discuss their future

---

Case Study 6   *Appealing against the loss of development rights in Sweden*

This case concerned a large landowner with property in a commune which was revising its local land-use plan. The argument of the lawyer representing the landowner was that the recommendations of the plan were not formulated according to the rules, and areas which were suitable for development were not zoned as such. The landowner argued that while he respected 'tradition', his farm could not be 'fossilised' – it was important to allow him to develop some land in order to sustain an effective agricultural operation. This would allow him to maintain the 'cultural landscape'.

The case was still in progress when the interview was carried out. However, the lawyer felt they were likely to be 'half successful' – some restrictions on development of the land had been lifted. This had followed intensive lobbying of local politicians (with the leaders of the two coalition parties being given a presentation at the landowner's country mansion). No lobbying of residents' or environmental protection groups had taken place.

---

proposals. According to the interviewee, 'they (the commune) help us; sometimes we help them'.

In contrast to Berkshire, South Paris and the E4 Corridor, a key element of Toulouse's planning process was a broad grouping of 88 major firms and organisations which had been established in the 1980s to promote the concept of the city as a 'technopole' (cf. Dreulle and Jalabert 1987). The partners included large 'hi-tech' companies (for example, Aérospatiale, Thomson CSF) and other businesses, developers, several local communes, major banks, research and development establishments, and higher education institutions. The objective of this grouping was to provide support for newly-established companies and companies relocating in the area, and to promote the development of greater Toulouse. There were also associations of communes and firms in the suburbs, which cooperated on urban planning and the economic promotion of the locality. One of these involved 33 communes and 360 firms.

Participation using the legal process

A crucial difference between the British planning system and those in Sweden and France is that individuals in the latter two countries are able to use the legal process to appeal against a draft local plan. As we have indicated, a Swedish *översiktsplan* has no legal standing and cannot be appealed against (although it is possible to appeal if the commune has an *översiktsplan* but has decided not make a land-use plan). Anyone who is affected by a land-use plan can, however, approach a special tribunal. This

---

Case Study 7
Use of the legal process to intervene in the Toulouse POS revision

Toulouse ProPOS and two local residents committees failed in their attempt to question the legality of the POS using a *recours grâcieux* ('official representation'). These groups subsequently attempted to get the POS partially annulled on the grounds of alleged irregularities in the way the plan was presented to the public. It was claimed that insufficient publicity had been available to local residents, that many of the detailed proposals presented at the inquiry were based on out-of-date plans and that the policy of intensification contradicted other policies, which stated that infilling had to be in character with neighbouring buildings and sufficient open space had to be preserved. None of these claims was accepted by the *tribunal administratif.*

---

includes landowners who feel their development rights have been 'sterilised' by zoning restrictions, although limits placed on this right mean that communes retain the balance of power and appeals are more frequently refused than accepted. The appeal is lodged with the county *(Län)* and the period before a decision is reached depends on the circumstances – this is usually at least nine months. The decision is then sent to the Department of Building and Planning for ratification. Case study 6 is an example of such an appeal. One interviewee – a planning lawyer – argued that many people only try to appeal when it is too late and:

> The secret is to be in on the discussions at the start of planning – communes are usually quite easy to talk to because they want to avoid the legal costs of appeal.

In France those affected by the content of a POS can appeal to an administrative tribunal. Plans can be annulled by a tribunal for a number of reasons. In one South Paris commune this was because an impact assessment had not been carried out. In other cases, non-conformity with the SDAU was cited as a reason for appeal.

While the possibility of protest to the courts exists, case study 7 illustrates how hard it is to appeal against a POS on the grounds of incompatibility with the SDAU. This is because it is not necessary for the two types of plan to conform exactly. In addition, because an SDAU is a long-term structure plan for a group of communes, the POS is the dominant plan in any given commune.

Conclusions
This chapter has examined public participation in plan formation in British, French and Swedish localities which have displayed rapid and extensive

growth over the last decade and more. Here, we draw conclusions about the similarities and differences in participation between these examples. Later, in Chapter 5, we will consider the wider implications of these findings, in terms of the relationship between government structures, planning systems and forms of participation.

There was a surprising degree of commonalty between the case-study areas in the ways participation occurred. To a large extent, public consultation tended to take place once the parameters of the structure or local plan had been established. This was a common complaint of residents' or other community groups, while the non-developer business community frequently complained that there were few mechanisms by which it could express its views adequately.

Another common feature was that access to local authority planning officers or politicians was seen by residents' and community groups as variable. Although some access was generally possible, groups felt that this was at least partially dependent on politicians' and planners' perceptions of the importance of consultation. The position was probably worse in France than in Britain or Sweden. In France, although mayors were on paper close to their public, there was a noticeable lack of information about planning policy.

In Sweden the importance of involvement in an officially-sanctioned interest group for successful participation was evident. On the other hand, the frequency of local elections meant that planning issues could relatively easily become part of the party political process.

An important difference between Britain and the other countries is the fact that the legal process may be used to question planning policy decisions. However, successful intervention using this channel was to a great extent dependent on an ability to show that the planning policy was illegal. This was difficult in both France and Sweden, because it required extensive knowledge of the planning system.

Notes
1. See Barlow and Duncan (1992; 1994) for further details of case-study areas.
2. National, local and regional elections are held every three years.

4 Public participation in the development-control process

In Chapter 2 we examined some of the main features of European planning systems. We identified a major difference between the British and continental European approaches to development control – the way planning permission is sanctioned. In Britain development-consent decisions are made on the basis of the matters contained in the local plan and any material considerations, whereas in most other countries zoning plans and ordinances give property owners the right to develop their land according to the specified norms. This implies that the British approach contains a considerable degree of discretion on the part of planning officers and local politicians. Although a form of zoning exists, inasmuch that consent can be relatively straightforward provided the proposals comply with the general parameters of the local plan, there is scope for disagreement, especially over the definition of 'material considerations'.

Although a zoning-based approach would appear – on paper at least – to afford greater certainty for developers, planners and individuals, it is equally possible that the award of development consent is subject to a degree of discretion. Healey (1990) notes that land-use zoning ordinances represent a set of rules established in an attempt to stamp out corrupt 'clientelist' practices. Although this may be the case, the proximity of local political networks to planning decision in some countries implies that an element of discretion also exists under zoning systems of planning. And in any case, the right to protest about specific development-consent decisions exists in most systems. In France individuals may apply for a form of outline planning permission (*certificat d'urbanisme*),[1] which specifies in broad terms what is proposed and what is acceptable to the commune. A full development consent (*permis de construire*) may subsequently be issued. However, at both stages the public, including third parties, is able to challenge the commune's decision. Similarly, in Sweden individuals and third parties are able challenge development consents.

In this chapter we therefore explore the way these different approaches enable or constrain public involvement in development decisions. There are two aspects to this form of 'participation' – the way the public is involved in the preparation or planning of development proposals and the extent to which protest can be made about decisions, by using the legal process. We then examine the implications of the different approaches – British and 'continental European' – for the success rate of applications for development.

Participation in the preparation of development proposals

Since July 1992 there have been statutory requirements for British local authorities to publicise all planning applications to allow neighbours and other interested parties to express their views. In a recent survey, Edmundson (1993) found that although over three-quarters of local authorities had changed their methods of publicity since the introduction of this requirement, only a third had committee-approved guidance concerning publicity and more than half had no guidance at all.

In major schemes development briefs are often used by authorities to specify certain requirements (for example, for affordable housing) as part of the grant of planning permission. In this way the description of what is required by the authority is built into the description of the proposed development. In principle, such an approach allows public discussion to shape what is included in these requirements, although planning briefs are informal guidance and carry less weight than local development plans. The use of development briefs also gives the local authority – and the public – a degree of control, inasmuch that development would be in breach of planning control if it were not implemented in accordance with the planning permission. However, public involvement in development proposals tends to occur more frequently during the period when the local authority is considering the application and negotiating for changes than during earlier or later phases of the planning process.

Nevertheless, despite official encouragement for greater public participation in development control, some commentators believe that the emphasis on the speed of decision-making, financial restrictions on local authorities, contracting-out and local government reorganisation may well undermine these moves (Edmundson 1993). In particular, Circular 15/92 advises local authorities to balance considerations of speed and cost of decision-making with providing the public with a reasonable opportunity to comment.

In Britain the degree of discretion in the development-control system therefore means that applicants for planning permission are not required to adhere precisely to the local plan or development brief. This results in the bargaining and negotiation which characterises the British system of development control. This discretionary approach thus affords objectors at least some prospect of an input into the process of preparing major development proposals. The approach in Sweden and France is fundamentally different. Broadly, the zoning system of development control in these countries means that the detailed agenda for discussion has largely been set by the developers and planners. This makes it hard for residents' groups or individuals to contribute to early discussions about a development proposal. On the other hand, appeals to legal tribunal against planning applications and consents can be made by third parties on an *a posteriori* basis.

In the Swedish case-study area, for example, the consensus of interviewees from residents' and other groups was that it is hard to significantly change development proposals once the detailed plan (see Chapter 3) has been established. While local residents and other interested parties are automatically consulted about proposals, it was felt to be essential to intervene as early as possible in the planning process to effect any changes. However, this was not always easy. As one interviewee put it, 'you have to be able to anticipate what is in the planners' minds'. On the other hand, planners felt that frequently people do not protest until they find out exactly what the plans involve. Underlying this is a basic contradiction, which to some extent undermines rights to consultation in development decisions – it is necessary to intervene early to modify proposals, but local residents frequently face a lack of information and/or experience in interpreting plans. In addition, the lack of detail in the early stages of proposals makes it harder to involve local interest.

This appeared to be a major problem under both the French and Swedish systems. In the latter, communes are obliged to provide details of proposals via a questionnaire and preliminary plan; groups and individuals then have one month to respond to the detailed proposals. Local residents' and other groups in one case-study commune had differing views on the degree to which consultation occurred. Registered groups were automatically approached by the commune whenever detailed new proposals are made. Unless they are registered with the commune, groups are not provided with details of proposals, although the commune holds quarterly meetings comprising all the residents' associations, the local branch of the *Naturskyddsföreningen* (a national environmental organisation), planners and the chair of the planning committee. However, some groups maintained that proposals were insufficiently detailed, making it hard to form an opinion, and there was a lack of support in interpreting planning applications (see case study 8).

Case Study 8   *Östra Barkaby*

Järfälla, a suburban commune north of Stockholm, was under considerable development pressure throughout the 1980s. This was partly the result of the regional plan for Stockholm, which directed the commune to increase the housing allocation in its local plan. The 1989-93 local plan envisaged growth occurring in a number of locations on the southern and western fringes of the commune, notably at Östra Barkaby. Much of the land for this scheme comprises a redundant military airfield; further land was bought by Järfälla from Stockholm commune. The eastern side of the site is a protected forest. The commune proposed to develop the site in stages for 2,500 - 3,000 new dwellings and office space for 3,000 employees. A new Ikea superstore was also proposed near to the Östra Barkaby site. As well as Östra Barkaby, several other major developments were proposed in the area.

A local residents' movement had emerged in 1987 largely from concern about general traffic levels in the area. There was also anxiety about the plans for the Ikea superstore, the existence of which, it was claimed, had been denied by local politicians for ten years. The fact that the superstore would have resulted in the demolition of a church resulted in the formation of an 'anti-superstore' political party, led by the local priest. It was agreed that there should be a division of labour between this political party and the main residents' group, Barkaby Trafik-föreningen, which had initially been involved in traffic issues but was now concerned about more general planning matters.

Another group, representing only 15 households immediately adjacent to the Östra Barkaby site, had similar origins. This had also initially been concerned about the volume of traffic but had subsequently shifted attention to noise pollution in general and the consequences of extra development for its part of the commune.

Neither of these groups was totally opposed to the Östra Barkaby scheme. The main concern for Barkaby Trafikföreningen was the balance between public and private transport, rather than the scheme itself. The smaller group argued that the main issue was 'the quality of life for children'.

Both groups felt that the details provided by the commune were not clear enough to enable them to form an opinion about proposals. There was also felt to be insufficient help in interpreting more technical points. As one interviewee put it, the commune automatically provided residents' and other groups with population, housing needs and traffic projections; but other than commenting that the scheme was too large because of the extra traffic generated and there should be more development on infill sites, they felt unable to respond further. The smaller residents' group had tried to overcome the problems caused by limited expertise by seeking the help of the chief planner and inviting local politicians to comment on the scheme. However, another local residents' group maintained that access to planners and politicians was variable, and depended largely on how significant they perceived the issue to be.

> At the time of the interviews detailed planning for Östra Barkaby had yet to begin and the slump in the property market had resulted in the proposals being scaled down. This meant that the interviewees were unable to assess the effect of their participation. The general consensus was that the scheme would be revised, meaning a further round of consultation. Residents' groups were therefore aiming to keep the issue alive until the next election in 1994.

These problems were more acute in the French case-study areas. Although there are rights to consultation and local residents have a fixed period (two months) in which to protest, there appeared to be considerable variety in the extent to which communes were prepared to cooperate in the provision of information about proposals. This was a particular problem in the Toulouse area, summed up in a report by a committee of residents' associations (*La Fédération des Oeuvres Laïques de Hauts-Garonne*) which outlined a number of obstacles to public participation:[2]

> ...minimal black and white notices (advertising public inquires) with small print... A public inquiry office as small as a postage stamp... delays in securing access to planning applications, sometimes a month to receive a photocopy! False and unchecked declarations in descriptions! Permits to demolish not attached to the site...

These problems are compounded by the French system by which outline planning applications (*certificats d'urbanisme*) can be back-dated to a previous POS. A *certificat d'urbanisme* lasts for one year and a construction permit is valid for two years. It is therefore possible for development to occur on the basis of the zoning rules in an older POS. This means that many *certificats d'urbanisme* are submitted by developers before a revision to a POS – there was a significant increase in the number of certificats before the 1989 revision of the Toulouse POS. This resulted in a doubling in planning applications in one year (see Table A1, Appendix 3).

These features of the French development-control system lead to severe problems for residents' groups wishing to protest about development proposals – the fact that a certificat or construction permit need not comply with a new POS can make it difficult to establish whether it is legal and thereby obtain a court injunction against development on the grounds of non-compliance.

The problems in participating on an *a posteriori* basis had generally led to close coordination between local groups. This helped maintain the spotlight on planning issues and provided a forum for the exchange of expertise and information. In Sweden, this coordination was to some extent built into the consultation system because of quarterly meetings held by

---

Case Study 9   The Bazacle residents' group

The Bazacle area of Toulouse borders the inner city and has been subject to intense development pressure for many years. This has involved the demolition of small houses and construction of large blocks of flats. In 1991 a collective of local residents' associations was established (the *Comité de Quartier Brienne-Bazacle-Amidonniers,* CQBBA). This was partly concerned about the loss of small houses and partly about proposals for a major new office and housing scheme.

The CQBBA is organised into a steering committee comprising six groups responsible for different issues (planning, open space, traffic etc). These liaise directly with the commune. One group is responsible for monitoring all outline planning applications. The CQBBA believes this system allows it to maintain clear relations with the Toulouse commune officials, as well as providing advance warning of any possible development schemes .

About a hundred residents belong to the organisation, although it was claimed that as many as 300 residents attend its general meetings and many non-members contact the committee with suggestions.

---

communes. However, several respondents – especially in France, but also in Sweden – said it was hard to build any kind of movement against planning proposals until concrete decisions were published. In this way, the lack of early information on proposals – and problems of interpretation – reinforced the lack of participation in development-control decisions, unless the scheme is especially large or controversial. Residents in some areas had, however, been politicised by previous events. In one case (in Sweden) a residents' association was preparing to protest about the commune's proposals for new housing by a lake – a local beauty spot – and associated new roads. The interviewee from this group said that residents had to some extent been politicised by a battle with the commune over land expropriation. This had enabled the association to set up a contact network with 15 other local groups and secure a weekly 15 minute phone-in slot on the local radio station. Case study 8 also illustrates how involvement by residents can grow from previous protest activities.

In France some residents' groups felt it was essential to monitor all planning applications, although we have seen how a lack of information can make this hard. One Toulouse residents' group did this and met monthly to decide how to respond. If necessary it would make an official request (*recour gracieux*) to the commune to obtain the details of the proposed scheme. In important cases representatives of the group would also try to meet the deputy mayor responsible for planning or the developer putting forward the proposal (case study 9).

Planners and local politicians in some of the case-study authorities regarded collaboration – within certain parameters – with the 'public' as a political resource. By liaising with public interest groups, they felt they could secure good public relations for official policies or proposals. Participation was viewed by planners as a way of reducing the likelihood of objections to planning applications. However, perhaps not surprisingly, liaison with specific interest groups – especially those representing local residents – appeared to be of greater significance to local authority representatives than liaison with promotional or cause-based groups, such as environmental or 'green' protest organisations. In one case, in Sweden, the local branch of the *Naturskyddsföreningen,* a national environmental group, had started a residents' group in an area where a new scheme was proposed, having been under the impression that their own submission had attracted relatively little interest from local politicians. On the other hand, a residents' group in the same commune argued that local politicians felt there was no need for such an organisation since it was their job to represent them.

In France there was a striking contrast between communes in which the local mayor was prepared to cooperate with local residents' groups – to a greater or lesser extent – and those in which mayors took the view that liaison was, at worst, unnecessary. While remaining common in very small communes, the view expressed by one south Paris mayor that there was no need to consult local residents about planning decisions because he 'knew everybody' (see Chapter 3), may be giving way to an acceptance of the need for limited participation. In Toulouse, the signing of a 'protocol' or planning agreement between the commune, developer and local residents' groups, after a period of relatively extensive consultation, may have signalled a new approach to participation in major schemes in that city (see case study 11, page 44). Nevertheless, even in situations where mayors and planners were prepared to engage in participation exercises, there was frequently a mismatch between the perception of local groups of what participation entails and that of local officers and politicians. Case study 10 illustrates this point, although it also shows that much depends on the specific personalities involved.

Participation using the legal process

We saw in Chapter 3 that a key difference between the British planning system and those in Sweden and France lies in the use of administrative law to appeal against planning decisions. In France, a representation to a *tribunal administratif* can be made only on grounds of non-conformity with the POS. It is not possible to protest about loss of amenity, although appeals

Case Study 10   ZAC Carnot, Massy

The commune of Massy lies 9 kms south of Paris, within the 'Axe Sud', a major growth zone. This is the focus for a large concentration of research and development organisations and 'high-tech' companies. Two regional railway lines, a high speed TGV railway line and three motorways have been built through Massy. In order to capitalise on this position and attract new office development, the Mayor of Massy (Claude Germon) persuaded French Railways (SNCF) to build a local TGV station, around which a major office development was proposed. A *société d'économie mixte* (SEM) – public-private joint venture company – was established to implement the scheme, known as the ZAC Carnot. The initial proposals (in November 1988) comprised 150,000 m^2 of offices, but by April 1989 the SEM was proposing 500,000 m^2 of offices and 3,268 dwellings. Subsequent discussions suggested that up to 1.5 million m^2 of office space could be built.

At the public inquiry there were 10,629 signatures against the scheme and only 22 in favour. Direct representations objecting to the proposals were made by 177 individuals or bodies. These included the councils and mayors of four neighbouring communes, which feared that all the disbenefits would be pushed on to them (personality clashes between mayors were also said to be an important factor).

The main pressure group in Massy is *Demain, Vivre à Massy-Palaiseau?* (DVMP). Planners from the SEM perceived this as a 'constructive' group and described it as 'essentially reformist' – broadly in favour of the scheme but seeking modifications. This was not, however, borne out in the interviews with DVMP representatives. In one manifesto the group argued that the creation of the Axe Sud was a major planning error because changes in telecommunications have rendered it unnecessary, Massy's TGV station is little used, the scheme borders the already-overdeveloped office sector in Hauts de la Seine, and it goes against the government's objectives of decentralisation from greater Paris. The manifesto points out that (author's translation, pp.2-3):

> One imagines that decisions of this nature and importance are the result of the analysis of experts and a coherent and reflective set of policies. The actual history of the project shows otherwise. It is hard to understand without putting the spotlight on the activities of the Mayor of Massy, M. Germon.

Initially, DVMP had a president who described his relations with the Mayor as 'very good'. However, DVMP's steering committee included members of the opposition on the local council. These were felt by the mayor to be 'too political' and DVMP believed this made it hard to obtain detailed information about the proposals. When the opposition members resigned from the local council, relations improved – the Mayor and SNCF began to take an interest in DVMP and the flow of information improved. The association now feels the mayor sees it as way of channelling information to the general public. Nevertheless, it believes that it is still only consulted after decisions have been taken on a specific development proposal – as one interviewee put it, 'if we have participated in any decisions, it's only because of our own efforts'. Obtaining information in advance of decisions was said to be still extremely hard.

As well as liaising with commune officials, DVMP has dealt with the *département*. This is mainly over specific points in the plans. According to DVMP, as soon as the politically centrist *département* council *(Conseil Géneral)* saw it was liaising with the socialist mayor, it wanted to talk. Nevertheless, DVMP believes that it is still 'up to (us) to prise information from the *(Conseil Géneral* and *Direction Départementale de l'Equipement)'*.

In general, DVMP feels its success can only be measured in terms of minor alterations to the development proposals. For example, a planned motorway bridge has been reduced in height and a link road has been realigned to pass through an industrial zone. DVMP's two (admitted) failures have been its inability to prevent the amount of proposed office space growing and its inability to criticise the proposed amount of housing, because it lacks the necessary skills to assess the housing impact of the employment growth.

---

can be made to a *tribunal civil*. However, appellants in these cases are required to pay expenses if they lose. Proving non-conformity is said to be hard. The back-dating of *certificats d'urbanisme,* described above, means that potential appellants frequently find it difficult to determine which POS is relevant. In any case, as was emphasised by several interviewees, an appeal requires a degree of expertise and knowledge that many groups, and most individuals, do not possess.

The process of appeal to a *tribunal administratif* can be protracted, slowing down the development process. Third parties with a direct interest have six months to appeal, while other objectors must appeal within two months. It can take two to three years for cases to be heard.

On the other hand, making a representation to a *tribunal administratif* generally freezes a proposal. Given the time taken to hear cases, this may well prompt a developer to negotiate, although only negotiations on details of schemes, such as car parking and external design, are permitted.

Broadly, though, residents' groups regarded the appeal process as too complicated and time-consuming. Nevertheless, the research found instances where residents' groups had succeeded in using a *tribunal administratif* to delay or modify schemes. In one example a group in Toulouse had succeeded in signing a 'protocol' with a developer to secure a package of planning gain, claimed to be the first in France (see case study 11, page 44). In a south Paris commune, a local association had been able to block a proposed office and housing scheme, bringing about the resignation of the mayor. However, it was more common for proposals to be modified or simply delayed (see case study 12, page 45).

Case Study 11   The ZAC de Bazacle, Toulouse

The proposed development site comprises four hectares of derelict buildings and vacant land between the River Garonne and a canal. The objective of the commune is to redevelop the site and open up the banks of the river to the public. In 1989 a decision was taken to create a ZAC for the area. This proposed 80,000 m^2 of housing (500 flats and student accommodation), together with retail and office space. The land was sold to a large national developer.

After preliminary discussions with local residents' associations in December 1990, the detailed planning of the ZAC was started. During this phase meetings were held between the developers and architects, the deputy mayor in charge of planning and the residents' associations. Help was received from the UCQ and *Toulouse ProPOS* (umbrella groups representing Toulouse's residents' associations. See case study 1, Chapter 3). Over ten further meetings between the CQBBA, the developers and the commune were held in 1992 and 1993. These also involved the city-wide umbrella groups, *Toulouse ProPOS,* UCQ, *les Amis de la Terre.*

The developers were initially very intransigent and threatened to go to court to force through the scheme. However, the CQBBA deposited objections with the *tribunal administratif,* on the grounds that the proposed development was bigger than that permitted by the POS. Prompted by the Mayor of Toulouse, the developers then started negotiating. This eventually resulted in a 'protocol' – essentially a planning agreement – between the developers, commune and CQBBA. This was claimed to be the first such agreement in France.

The CQBBA was able to negotiate an 8,000 m^2 reduction in the built-space of the scheme. In addition, the protocol established conditions on the amount of open space, 'social facilities' (500 m^2 was set aside for a crèche, dispensary and meeting area) and a promenade along the canal.

To some extent, the CQBBA believes the developers hands were forced, since the mayor was in favour of a negotiated agreement, and as long as the objections remained on deposit with the tribunal administratif construction was unable to start.

Generally, the protocol is regarded as a success – according to the interviewee, other associations have now said they are keen to enter similar agreements and local developers see this as a way of reducing the amount of time spent planning a scheme.

Planning by appeal and the development process

We noted in the introduction to this chapter that a zoning-based approach to development control potentially offers greater certainty to developers than the more discretionary British system. However, the proximity of local political networks to planning decisions and the right of individuals to protest about decisions may well undermine this certainty. In order to explore the level of certainty in development-control decisions under the

---

Case Study 12   ZAC Carnot, Massy

With the help of a local lawyer – himself a member of a residents' protest group in a neighbouring commune – *Demain, Vivre à Massy-Palaiseau?* (a pressure group formed to fight the Massy development) approached the *Tribunal Administratif* to have the initial ZAC proposals annulled. This appeal was granted in February 1992 because the Tribunal held that the scheme was incompatible with the existing SDAU for the region. However, the proposals were subsequently modified and approved by the local council in June 1993. One member of a residents' group in a neighbouring commune claimed that the new proposals have just as significant implications for Palaiseau as the previous scheme and they are seen by their own politicians as a 'provocation'. This group has now made representations to the *Tribunal Administratif* on the grounds that the proposals are still incompatible with the SDAU. A decision had yet to be made at the time of interview.

---

different approaches, we examined annual data on planning permissions for housebuilding in the British and French case-study areas. This comprised data on the total number of planning applications, the number of applications granted permission, the number withdrawn and, for Berkshire, the number granted on appeal. We believed that under the more discretionary British system, it was possible that fewer applications would be granted.

Unfortunately, it was not possible to obtain equivalent data for the E4 Corridor. However, planners here said that the refusal of planning permission was virtually unheard of. This was because developers would not seek consent for schemes which failed to conform with the zoning arrangements, although planners also claimed that many developers would attempt to renegotiate the zoning requirements in their favour.

In both the French case-study areas the increasing use of appeals appears to be reflected in a declining success rate of development applications. Data on planning permits for new housing were obtained for all the communes in the South Paris and Toulouse areas (Appendix 3). In general, there is a very low rate of refusals, compared to the British case-study area (Table 1). In Toulouse no applications were refused permission in the period from 1980 to 1988. In South Paris the refusals rate is higher and has persistently grown, but the proportion of applications which are turned down remains low.

Table 1   Success rates of residential planning applications

Percentages

Year	Berkshire* refused	Berkshire* withdrawn	South Paris refused	South Paris withdrawn	Toulouse refused	Toulouse withdrawn
1980					0.0	2.9
1981	37.7	4.5			0.0	5.6
1982	38.3	3.5			0.0	3.2
1983	34.4	3.8			0.0	5.0
1984	38.1	4.5			0.0	1.1
1985	34.8	4.5			0.0	6.4
1986	35.9	4.1	4.3	3.1	0.0	6.1
1987	35.9	6.8	4.7	2.6	0.0	7.5
1988	49.3	7.7	4.6	2.5	0.0	11.6
1989	32.7	4.7	5.6	3.0	6.2	3.9
1990	29.6	4.8	6.8	2.4		
1991	28.1	3.5	6.9	3.5	3.0	7.0
1992	23.1	3.1				

Source: Direction Départementale de l'Equipement (Toulouse); Direction Régionale de l'Equipement (South Paris); Berkshire County Council; district councils

*   Bracknell, Newbury, Wokingham. Reading not available.

It is also important to take into account the withdrawal of planning applications. In France developers tend to negotiate with the planning authorities (and occasionally local residents' groups) before the decision and unfavourable comments may lead to a withdrawal (Booth 1989). As Table 1 shows, there was no clear trend towards an increase in the already very low rate of withdrawals in either of the French case-study areas. It would have been useful to obtain data on the refusal rates for *certificats d'urbanisme* (outline planning permissions), since these indicate the authority's attitude towards the principle of development on a site. Unfortunately, it was not possible to obtain these data at the required spatial scale.

In contrast, the more discretionary nature of the British development-control system is reflected in the rate of refusals in Berkshire. As Table 1 shows, about a third of applications were turned down each year in the 1980s; there seems to have been a reduction in the success rate of residential applications since the 1970s (Table 2, page 47).[3] This may partly be the result of developers making more 'speculative' applications during phases

Table 2   **The declining success rate of residential planning applications in selected Berkshire districts**

	per cent of all residential applications	
	1974-81	1982-88
Newbury	63.2	53.5
Wokingham	51.8	53.4
Bracknell	60.2	53.6

Source: 1982-88 derived from planning applications database, Berkshire County Council planning department; 1974-81 from Short et al (1986: Table A2.4)

of rapid growth, such as the mid 1980s. When there is a prospect of inflation in house and land prices developers tend to adopt a more confrontational approach and make more unacceptable applications, in order to 'test' the limits of the system. This may be borne out in that the proportion of permissions granted *on appeal* has generally risen during the 1980s (Table 3).

Another factor leading British developers to behave more speculatively in the 1980s may have been their perception that planning policy was undergoing 'liberalisation' at the hands of central government. In Berkshire this was justified – between 1980 and 1988 in Reading alone nearly 70,000 m^2 of office space was allowed on appeal, and by August 1988 four of

Table 3   **Permissions granted after appeal as a share of all applications, 1981-88**

	per cent of all residential applications		
	Bracknell	Newbury	Wokingham
1981	4.3	2.4	3.6
1982	10.1	3.6	3.0
1983	4.6	1.8	6.7
1984	7.5	3.3	3.8
1985	14.0	5.5	7.8
1986	2.8	5.2	8.7
1987	8.3	5.0	11.3
1988*	5.8	2.7	1.5

Source: derived from planning applications database, Berkshire County Council planning department.

*   18.9 per cent of planning applications in Bracknell, 19.2 per cent of those in Newbury, and 14.6 per cent of those in Wokingham were undecided at the year end.

Berkshire's six districts had breached the limits for office space set by the 1984-96 structure plan. Dr John Cunningham, Labour's then environment spokesman, claimed that local authorities were passing plans for development which they did not approve of simply because they could not afford to fight appeals which they may lose (*Reading Evening Post*, 20 June 1988).

Speculative 'testing' of the system may also be seen in the Massy-Saclay-Palaiseau area of South Paris. This was subject to considerable development pressure in the 1980s by speculative developers (Barlow and Duncan 1994) and had a higher refusal rate than the two new towns, where the land market was more tightly controlled.

Conclusions

The previous chapter explored ways in which the public and business community participated in plan formation in the British, French and Swedish case-study areas. In this chapter we turned to public participation in specific proposals for development.

One implication of the British, 'discretionary', approach is that there are potentially more opportunities for the public to intervene in the development process – as well as intervention when major proposals are under discussion, especially when development briefs are used, intervention can occur in the form of objections to published planning applications. Zoning-based systems, on the other hand, potentially offer a greater degree of certainty to developers, inasmuch that development proposals which comply with the zoning arrangements are – at least in theory – granted automatically. However, we also noted that a degree of discretion was likely to exist in some countries with zoning approaches to development control, because of the close relationships between local political networks and local planning systems. In addition, third-party rights of protest were also a feature of many zoning-based systems.

The research found that in terms of the 'certainty' of obtaining planning permission there were indeed major differences between the British approaches, on the one hand, and those of France and Sweden. Data on the proportion of planning applications which were granted consent showed that refusal of permission was extremely rare in the latter countries. In the British case-study area, however, not only was refusal considerably more common, but it appeared that refusal rates had grown during the 1980s. However, this picture does not account for the negotiation that occurs before applications are submitted in France and Sweden. In these countries discussions with planning authorities would frequently take place prior to the submission of a detailed application. Pre- and post-application negotiations also occur in the British system, but here it is also common for developers to make 'speculative' applications to 'test' local planning attitudes in the British case-study area.

A rise in refusal rates in the two French case-study areas could also be detected towards the end of the 1980s – this may have been the result of increased use of the legal process to protest about development proposals. Nevertheless, the appeal process was generally seen as far too complicated and time-consuming.

In all three countries, planners and local politicians appeared to regard collaboration with the 'public' as a political resource to be mobilised when seeking consent for planning applications. Planners saw participation as a way of reducing the likelihood of objections to specific development proposals. However, this collaboration occurred within parameters established by the planning system itself and by the attitudes of local politicians and planning officers.

Another problem faced by those wishing to participate in the development-control process was their lack of experience in interpreting plans. This was compounded in some cases by a lack of information in specific planning applications. The lack of detail available in the early stages of proposals appeared to make it harder to encourage public interest in becoming involved in participation, which in turn meant it was often harder to intervene early enough to modify proposals.

Notes

1. There are two forms of *certificat d'urbanisme,* depending on the degree of detail provided in the application.
2. In *Enjeu 31,* No. 23, December 1991, p.3, author's translation.
3. It should be noted that the figures for the most recent period may have slightly undercounted successful applications because the number of yet-to-be-decided applications rises in more recent years.

5 Conclusions: The politics of urban development

Introduction
Two sets of conclusions can be drawn from the research on participation in Britain, France and Sweden. First, we need to consider the reasons for differences and similarities in participation between the three countries. Specifically, to what extent do the concepts of 'growth coalitions' and 'urban regimes' help us to understand the politics of urban development; what is the relationship between the broad 'decision rules' of planning systems, the features of each national approach to planning and the ways in which participation takes place?

Second, we need to draw conclusions on the implications of the findings from the three countries for policy on planning participation in Britain - can lessons be learnt for front-line workers involved in participation exercises; do different approaches to participation have implications for planning 'efficiency'; to what extent will a more 'plan-led' system in Britain result in changes to the nature of participation?

Urban-development politics
We argued in Chapter 1 that research on 'growth coalitions' and 'urban regimes' provides a possible tool for understanding the ways in which the variety of groups with an interest in urban-development interact. We emphasised that the focus of this literature has tended to be on the privileged position of business in urban-planning systems and the desire of property-based interests to capture increased land values arising from urban planning. There has also been discussion about the emergence of anti-development activity as a response to local growth coalitions. The question we need to address here is whether this research can help explain the differences between and within the three systems.

There was clearly pro-development pressure in all the case-study areas, either in the form of participation in plan formation or development control, or more direct lobbying. However, the principal actors, the functional relations between them, and their primary motives varied considerably.

Certainly, property-related interests were closely involved in the planning process at all stages. Indeed, in the British and Swedish cases landowners and developers were perhaps the only distinctive lobby. However, these did not have any organisational links with the rest of the business community. In south Paris property developers were also important in promoting development through the planning process, but the distinguishing feature here was the role played by local authorities – especially their mayors – as the primary force behind local 'boosterism'.

However, these groupings cannot be described as 'coalitions', nor do they represent 'policy communities' – they are not especially integrated and there is only limited interaction between their participants. Moreover, even in Toulouse, where arguably there is an identifiable and coherent coalition bringing together local authorities, land and developer interests, the broader business community and other bodies, it is not evident that property interests are necessarily the leading participants. The Toulouse coalition is, however, distinctive because it represents a grouping of vested interests concerned with promoting the conditions for local growth and seeking to build on indigenous entrepreneurial strengths.

While business interests, developers and landowners in the other case-study areas also clearly participated in the local planning system, this tended to occur largely on an individual basis through representations made at local plan inquiries or over specific development proposals. In the E4 Corridor, for example, large local employers were consulted automatically in the local plan process and the national employers federation intervened at the regional and national level. Similarly, in Berkshire major local employers and the chambers of commerce intervened in the planning process. However, it was hard to distinguish any *coherent* grouping of business interests. It was the provision of infrastructure which appeared to most exercise local business representatives; participation was essentially *ad hoc* and responsive to specific issues and there appeared to be very little open-ended discussion with local authorities about general urban policy.

Turning to intervention in the urban-development process by members of the public and their representatives, it is clear that the protection of existing 'use values' was the primary force behind participation. There was concern in particular to protect the existing 'quality' of the neighbourhood, usually expressed in terms of traffic volume and loss of open space. However, in neither the French nor the Swedish case-study areas can 'nimbyism' be described as a direct protest against the adverse effects of development on house prices. This, it will be recalled, is held to be one factor behind anti-development protest. In the E4 Corridor and Toulouse, where house prices were relatively stable or even declining in the 1980s, this is perhaps to be expected. However, even in south Paris and Berkshire, where prices were high and there had been rapid inflation, residents' groups claimed not to be especially concerned about the effect of new development on the monetary value of their housing. Again, there was little open-ended discussion between planners and residents' groups about general urban-development policy, although this was perhaps more prominent in Berkshire. Most participation took the form of a response to specific issues, whether these were local plan amendments or individual development proposals.

The relationship between residents' groups and planning officials and politicians found in the case-study areas lends some weight to Stone's (1989) argument that urban regimes perform an empowering and coordinating role for their members. To some extent, the official sanctioning of certain groups, which are brought into participation exercises, suggests that planning officials see participation as a way of managing interest groups. This is perhaps more developed in Britain and Sweden than France. In Berkshire and the E4 Corridor the participatory framework is comparatively formalised and there is a prevalent ideology of planners as 'mediators'. In Toulouse, however, the use of planning 'protocols' is now seen by local politicians as a way of bringing community groups 'on board', but the balance of power remains with the pro-development lobby and urban-development politics remains essentially confrontational. And in South Paris, communes and their mayors have merely granted small-scale planning gains to offset protest about the scale of development.

To summarise, the research suggests there are similarities between the case-study areas in terms of the relationship between the public and business communities and the planning process. Business involvement is generally restricted (apart from that by developers and landowners); protest by local residents is largely about quality-of-life issues. In both cases, involvement in urban-development politics is largely reactive rather than pro-active. The lack of identifiable 'growth coalitions' or 'urban regimes' in Britain or Sweden does not, of course, mean that the structure of local government, government-industry relations or urban planning prevents them from emerging. Such coalitions have been shown to exist in Britain (see Harding 1991; Newman 1994).

The main difference between the case-study areas lies in the extent to which participation occurs. In all three countries similar problems of participation for local residents and businesses existed, despite the different planning systems. Perhaps most noticeable was the relative lack of participation in planning decision-making in both the French case study areas. While planning officials and local politicians in all three countries to some extent saw participation as a way of legitimising policies and decisions, in Toulouse and south Paris it was distinctly muted.

To *explain* these differences we must consider the way alternative approaches to planning operate in practice. Clearly, the British, French and Swedish planning systems each have specific regulations about when and how participation is allowed, and who can be involved. These regulations are, however, situated within a broader framework of 'decision rules' and are also open to local interpretation.

Decision-making 'rules' and the local context

We argued in Chapters 1 and 2 that public participation in the urban-development process is likely to be influenced by a combination of factors. Some of these are the result of constraints imposed by the broad structural features of planning and government systems; some are the result of the local context within which urban planning occurs.

In Chapter 1 we suggested there were important differences between Britain, France and Sweden in terms of the dominant 'rules' by which planning systems operate. British development planning can, for example, be characterised as a system based on semi-judicial processes. These involve the legal and administrative definition of interests around a specified agenda. Debate, under this model, is relatively open, with decisions being agreed on the basis of fairness and reasonableness. In contrast, the French approach to planning tends towards a bureaucratic-legal model, whereby interests may well be legally and administratively defined, but debate revolves around the correct use of formal procedures. Decisions are made according to predetermined rules. The Swedish approach involves open democratic debate, albeit one which is politically and ideologically determined. The terms of entry to this debate are officially sanctioned. Under this framework decisions are solved by broad agreement between the officially sanctioned parties.

As well as broad structural differences between national planning and government systems, participation in urban planning will be influenced by locally contingent factors. However, the relative importance of local context may vary. By local context, we are referring to such factors as the techniques used by planners to elicit participation, the stage in the development process the public becomes involved, the degree to which specialist knowledge is required to understand the implications of a plan or specific development proposal, and whether the plan or proposal has an immediate tangible impact.

The importance of broad structural factors and local context is evident in the French case studies. For example, participation in planning decision-making is constrained by a legal framework which closely specifies which issues the public or organisations can comment on. As we have seen, despite wide membership of chambers of commerce, business involvement is limited and protest via the judicial system is highly formalised. However, the French system also contains elements of 'clientelism'. Urban-development politics frequently involve negotiation between commune mayors, the *préfets* of *départements* and developers. While the patron-client dependency of other countries is, perhaps, less evident in French urban-development politics today than in the past, the importance of individual politicians in planning decisions is clear from the case studies. This is an inevitable by-product of the very small scale of communes and the increased powers given to mayors in the early 1980s.

In Sweden, the discursive approach to planning, in which the terms of entry are broadly negotiated at a national level, also comes out in the case studies. Under this framework, individual participation is co-opted into a broader form of participation involving legitimised interest groups. Input by these groups in the pre-participation phase of the planning process is necessary for successful intervention. Furthermore, certain actors, such as the national housing co-operatives, have a privileged position in the planning decision-making process.

Finally, the semi-judicial British approach, whereby an independent planning inspector is appointed to mediate in plan-formation decisions, has arguably faced growing tensions in the 1980s. On the one hand, central government has moved to push planning decision-making further down the administrative scale. On the other hand, central government has exerted firmer control over the activities of local authorities through the granting of planning consents on appeal. This led to increasing conflict in the planning system, with participation taking the form of protest by pressure groups representing different interests. Debate took place in a relatively open, but increasingly adversarial form. This pattern was to some extent replicated in decision-making about development consents.

The importance of local context is also clear from the degree to which planners and politicians felt collaboration with potential protesters was important. For example, it was surprising that in Sweden – with its nationally established rules and norms – there were such distinct differences between communes in terms of the relationship between planners and politicians and interest groups, depending on the former group's perception of the importance of participation.

To summarise, the findings suggest that while the local context is a crucial dimension for understanding differences in urban-development politics, it is also necessary to consider the constraints imposed by broader structural features. In particular, the national approach to planning and development control clearly influences the way public participation occurs. Under the British system there appear to be more opportunities for the public to intervene, since objections can occur through representations made at the structure and local plan stages and through objections in relation to specific planning applications. This may be one factor behind the higher failure rate of planning applications in Berkshire. It is also clear that there is an element of post-plan protest in France, despite the zoning approach to development control. The position in Sweden can perhaps be described as intermediate. In the E4 Corridor, intervention by local residents occurs largely at the plan-making stage, as in France, while the mechanisms for participation are similar to those of the UK.

There is, however, no clear relationship between the extent of local government financial autonomy and patterns of development politics, as was suggested in Chapter 1. Local government in Britain and Sweden lies at two poles in terms of financial autonomy, but local authorities in both countries were equally concerned about the costs of growth. French communes gained more financial autonomy during the 1980s, along with greater powers to control or promote growth. In addition, commune syndicates are now able to harmonise and redistribute taxes in order to overcome the problem of small-scale government units. Nevertheless, many communes in the case-study areas were just as concerned as their British counterparts about the costs of growth.

Lessons for planning participation in the UK

Although there is debate about its legal implications (Purdue 1994), section 54A of the Town and Country Planning Act 1990 has elevated the status of local plans and has been seen as a shift towards a more 'plan-led' framework. The new approach emphasises that development-control decisions should be taken in accordance with the policies in the local plan. Purdue (1994) points out that since policies will be material in almost all development proposals, section 54A will apply to the majority of planning applications. This suggests that adequate public input into the policy-formation stages of local plans will be essential for democratic representation – provided a planning application conforms with the appropriate policies, the granting of consent may become more of a formality. In this sense, it could be argued that British planning has moved towards a zoning-based approach, as found in France or Sweden.

As we have seen, in these countries very few planning applications are refused consent, although rights to protest through the administrative courts are built into their planning systems. The evidence from the three countries echoes other research in showing that public involvement in plan-formation stages tend to be limited. Edmundson (1993) shows that section 54A has stimulated the involvement of landowners, developers and other businesses, rather than the general public, in plan-formation. The French case studies show that there was relatively little participation in plan-formation by members of the public. It is, however, clear that this is not an *inevitable* feature of planning systems – there was more widespread consultation in the Swedish case-study areas, although even here there were familiar problems associated with a lack of public understanding of more abstract plans, compared to more immediate and site-specific proposals.

What, then, are the implications of these findings for participation in the British planning system? Two conflicting tendencies appear to be at work in Britain. On the one hand, there is greater concern on the part of government about participation. Since July 1992 there has been legislation requiring third-party views to be consulted, so that 'neighbours and other interested parties can make their views known'. Local authorities are now required to publicise applications which, *inter alia,* depart from the development plan or are subject to environmental assessment. Major and minor applications must be publicised by site notices and/or letters to adjoining occupiers.

Arguably, the agenda behind recent moves towards increased public participation is related to the government's emphasis on 'customer power', of which the planning element of the citizen's charter is a manifestation.

Reinforcing these moves towards greater participation is concern in the EC to encourage transparency for local property markets, in which planning systems are seen as a form of non-tariff barrier to transnational investment. As Healey and Williams (1993: 701) put it:

> Planning systems may have significant effects in promoting or limiting development opportunities, and discriminating between 'insiders' and 'outsiders' in access to these.

They conclude that while the EC cannot expect to transform national legal systems and political cultures by direct intervention,[1] it may well influence the development of national approaches to planning.

On the other hand, these trends must be weighed against concern about the efficiency of planning. In particular, the government and DOE wish to speed up public inquiries into local plans. Indeed, the key performance criteria for both the government and DOE would appear to be the achievement of 'value for money'. Circular 15/92 advises local authorities to balance considerations of speed and cost of decision-making with providing the public with a reasonable opportunity to comment.

Although a detailed analysis of the speed of the planning process was beyond the scope of this project, anecdotal evidence suggested that securing development consent for larger schemes was often faster in France or Sweden than the UK. On the other hand, a zoning approach does not necessarily mean greater *certainty* – and thus more efficiency – for developers, landowners or planners. It is clear that a degree of negotiation between developers and planners often occurs in France and Sweden in the pre-application stage, although the level of uncertainty for developers is probably lower than in Britain. This, in turn, has a number of implications for the business strategies of developers and knock-on effects on profit margins and land prices: the more 'uncertain' British system appears to encourage more speculative behaviour (cf. Barlow and King 1992).

What may emerge in the next decade is not a 'continental style' zoning approach to planning. While there has been a move towards a plan-led approach, the new framework does not mean that British local plans represent binding legal documents, as found in most other European countries. A local plan will remain only one of the material considerations in the award of planning permission, albeit one which has gained in importance. There will still be scope for discretion in interpreting policies and in deciding which of two or more conflicting policies should take precedence.[2] Edmundson (1993) argues that section 54A is unlikely to reduce the scope of public involvement in the processing of planning applications. One reason for this is the possibility that the presumption in favour of local plans by the courts will not rise markedly (cf. Purdue 1994). Furthermore, the primacy of local plans is also strongly influenced by government policy – rigid policies are discouraged by DOE intervention in the plan-making process; Planning Policy Guidance Note 1 states that local plan policies do not take precedence over government policies; and plans may be superseded by more recent guidance.

The 'uncertainty' resulting from a planning system which relies heavily on discretion may well turn government increasingly to support a 'partnership' approach, at least for larger development and infrastructure schemes. The partnership model, such as that emerging in projects proposed under the Single Regeneration Budget, may be more appealing to government than increased direct 'participation' because it is probably easier to manage the 'stakeholders' and the way they interact.

Some practical conclusions

To what extent can the findings of this study provide practical conclusions for those involved in planning? A number of points can be made. First, the research shows that early involvement by the public in the planning process is essential for smooth decision-making. One of the most common causes of delay and conflict is the failure of planners, developers and the public to communicate adequately – frequently public involvement is too late to allow any option other than opposition. As Cowan (1993) notes, the planning process is unusual in the degree to which it is a statutory process in which political decisions are taken in the light of professional advice. The extent and quality of public input are therefore important influences on the quality of planning decisions.

Second, we can echo the principles for front-line workers involved in participation put forward by Wilcox (1994a and b). In particular, it is important for those charged with managing participation to be clear about their objectives, whether these are the provision of information, testing opinions, inviting fresh ideas, or helping people to achieve their aims. It is also important for planners to maintain an appropriate balance between keeping control and gaining public support, and to ensure that they are able to deliver their promises.

Third, the case studies found that a range of different techniques for participation were used by planning authorities. These included exhibitions, surveys, public meetings, and simulations. More successful exercises in participation, however, tended to involve smaller group discussions with the various interest groups. These allowed agendas to be established and mutual trust to emerge, before wider public meetings were held. We also saw how informal contact between planning authorities, local politicians and different community interests can be important, although this should not be to the extent that other interests are excluded. The concept of 'planning aid' has a part to play is this process. Local authorities increasingly recognise that a planning-aid service can complement their own attempts to communicate with the public by giving independent advice (Cowan 1993).

Epilogue

As Stone (1989) notes, a fundamental problem for local residents is that they are a diffuse group with only a limited means of interaction with elected officials – contact between voters and elected officials tends to be shallow and is frequently ephemeral. This can mean that democratic participation in urban-development decisions is limited.

'Participation' is clearly needed to secure acquiescence for planning decisions; there is perhaps a growing need for participation to be seen as effective. The research shows, however, that similar problems of achieving participation for local residents and businesses exist, despite the different approaches that have been adopted. The achievement of equitable policy-making and implementation therefore appears to be a universally elusive goal.

Notes
1. It has been argued that intervention in planning systems breaches subsidiarity principles.
2. MacDonald (1994) notes that this makes a local plan only as good as the information it is based on and hence vulnerable to a loss of relevance and credibility over time.

References

Adams, D., May, H. and Pawson, G. (1990) 'The distribution of influence at local plan inquiries'. *Planning Outlook* 33(2), pp.133-135.

Adams, D. and Pawson, G. (1992) 'Local plan inquiries'. *The Planner* 4 September, pp.12-14.

Agnew, J. (1981) 'Homeownership and the capitalist social order'. In M. Dear and A. Scott (eds.) *Urbanization and Urban Planning in Capitalists Society.* New York, Methuen.

Alterman, R. (1982) 'Planning for public participation: the design of implementation strategies'. *Environment and Planning B* 9(4).

Alterman, R., Harris, D. and Hill, M. (1984) 'The impact of public participation on planning. The case of the Derbyshire Structure Plan'. *Town Planning Review* 55(2), pp.177-196.

Alty, D. and Darke, R. (1991) 'A city centre for the people: involving the community in planning for Sheffield's central area'. In V. Nadin and J. Doak (eds.) *Town Planning Responses to the Changing City.* Aldershot, Gower.

Ashford, D. (1983) 'The Socialist reorganization of French local government – another Jacobin reform?' *Environment and Planning C* 1: 29-44.

Ball, A. and Millard, F. (1986) *Pressure Politics in Industrial Societies.* London, Macmillan

Barlow, J. (1990) 'Who plans Berkshire? The housing market, house price inflation and developers'. *Centre for Urban and Regional Research Working Paper* No. 72.

Barlow, J. (1993) 'Controlling the housing land market: some examples from Europe'. *Urban Studies* 30(7): 1129-1149.

Barlow, J. (1995) 'The politics of urban growth. "Boosterism" and "nimbyism" in boom regions'. *International Journal of Urban and Regional Research* (forthcoming).

Barlow, J. and Duncan, S. (1992) Markets, states and housing provision: four European growth regions compared. *Progress in Planning* 38(2): 93-177.

Barlow, J. and King, A. (1992) 'The state, the market and competitive strategy. Housebuilding in the UK, France and Sweden'. *Environment and Planning A* No.24:381-400.

Barlow, J. and Duncan, S. (1994) *Success and Failure in European Housing Provision.* Oxford, Pergammon.

Barlow, J. and Savage, M. (1986) 'The politics of growth: cleavage and conflict in a Tory heartland'. *Capital and Class* No.30: 156-182.

Bennett, R., Krebs, G. and Zimmermann, H. (eds.) (1993) *Chambers of Commerce in Britain and Germany and the Single European Market.* London, Anglo-German Foundation.

Bennett, R., Wicks, P. and McCoshan, A. (1994) *Local Empowerment and Business Services.* London, UCL Press.

Best, J. and Bowser, L. (1986) 'A people's plan for Central Newham'. *The Planner* 72(11), pp.21-25.

Boaden, N., Goldsmith, M., Hampton, W. and Stringer, P. (1980) 'Planning and participation in practice. A study of public participation in structure planning'. *Progress in Planning* 13(1/2).

Booth, P. (1989) 'How effective is zoning in the control of development?' *Environment and Planning B* 16: 401-415.

Booth, P. (1993) 'The cultural dimension in comparative research: making sense of development control in France'. *European Planning Studies* 1(2): 217-229.

Bruton, M.; G. Crispin; P. Fidler; E. Hill (1982) 'Local plans PLIs in practice'. *The Planner* 68(1 and 2), pp.16-18 and 50-51.

Cameron-Blackhall, J. (1994) 'Simplified Planning Zones (SPZs) or simply political zeal?' *Journal of Planning and Environment Law,* February, pp.117-123.

Castles, F. (1978) *The Social Democratic Image of Society.* London, RKP.

Cheshire, P., d'Arcy, E. and Giussani, B. (1992) 'Purpose built for failure? Local, regional and national government in Britain'. *Environment and Planning C* 10.

Cohen, J. (1985) 'Strategy or Identity: New Theoretical Paradigms and Contemporary Social Movements' in *Social Research* 52(4)

Cowan, R. (1993) 'Planning aid climbs of the professional margins'. *Planning* No.1040, 15 October, pp.22-23.

Cox, K. (1991a) 'Questions of abstraction in studies in the new urban politics'. *Journal of Urban Affairs* 13(3): 267-280.

Cox, K. (1991b) 'The abstract, the concrete and the argument in the new urban politics'. *Journal of Urban Affairs* 13(3): 299-306.

Cox, K. and Mair, A. (1989) 'Book review essay'. *International Journal of Urban and Regional Research* 13(1): 137-146.

Coxall, W. (1986) *Parties and Pressure Groups.* London, Longman.

Dear, M. (1992) 'Understanding and overcoming the NIMBY syndrome'. *Journal of the American Planning Association* 58, pp.288-299.

Dreulle, S. and Jalabert, G. (1987) 'La technopole Toulousaine; le développement de la Vallée de l'Hers'. *Espace Géographique* 1: 15-29.

Duncan, S. and Goodwin, M. (1987) *Uneven Development and the Local State.* London, Methuen,

Edmundson, T. (1993) 'Public demands right to say where control show pinches'. *Planning* No.1046, 26 November, pp.22-23.

Elander, I. and Strömberg, T. (1992) 'Whatever happened to Social Democracy and planning? The case of local land and housing policy in Sweden'. In Lundqvist, L. (ed.) *Policy, Organisation, Tenure. A Comparative History of Small Welfare States.* Scandinavian Housing and Planning Research Supplement No.2. Oslo and Stockholm, Scandinavian University Press.

Fainstein, S. (1991) 'Rejoinder to: Questions of abstraction in studies in the new urban politics'. *Journal of Urban Affairs* 13(3): 281-287.

Forsberg, H. (1991) 'Central-local relations in Swedish Acts on physical planning. A historical review'. *Scandinavian Housing and Planning Research* 8.

Friedland, R. (1983) *Power and Crisis in the City.* Basingstoke, Macmillan.

Galliano D. (1987) 'Groupes industriels et territoire: un rapport en mutation. L'exemple de la technopole toulousaine'. *Revue d'Economie Régionale et Urbaine* No.3.

Galliano D. and Gilly J. (1987) 'Toulouse technopôle et la région Midi-Pyrénées: des disparités structurelles croissantes'. *Statistiques et Etudes Midi-Pyrénées* No.4: 9-13.

Gleeson, B. and Memon, P. (1994) 'The NIMBY syndrome and community care facilities: a research agenda for planning'. *Planning Practice and Research* 9(2): 105-118.

GMA Planning, PE International, Jaques and Levis (1993) *Integrated Planning and the Granting of Permits in the European Community.* London, HMSO.

Goodchild, B.; Y. Gorrichon; L. Bertrand (1993) 'Local housing strategies in France'. *Planning Practice and Research* 8(1): 4-8.

Hall, P., Breheny, M., McQuaid, R. and Hart, D. (1987) *Western Sunrise. The Genesis and Growth of Britain's Major High Tech Corridor.* London: Allen and Unwin.

Hampton, W. and Walker, R. (1978) 'The individual citizen and public participation'. *Linked Research Project into Public Participation in Structure Planning,* Interim Paper No.13. Department of Extra Mural Studies, University of Sheffield.

Harding, A. (1991) 'The rise of urban growth coalitions, UK-style?' *Environment and Planning C* 9: 295-317.

Healey, P. (1990) 'Policy processes in planning'. *Policy and Politics* 18(1), pp. 91-103.

Healey, P., MacNamara, P., Elson, M. and Doak, J. (1988) *Land Use PLanning and the Mediation of Urban Change.* Cambridge, Cambridge University Press.

Healey, P. and Williams, R. (1993) 'European planning systems: diversity and convergence'. *Urban Studies* 30(4/5), pp.701-720.

Heclo, H. and Madsen, H. (1987) *Policy and Politics in Sweden. Principles and Pragmatism.* Philadelphia, Temple University Press.

Jaffe, M. and Smith, T. (1986) *Siting Group Homes for Developmentally Disabled Persons.* Chicago, American Planning Association.

Keating, M. (1991) *Comparative Urban Politics. Power and the City in the United States, Canada, Britain and France.* Aldershot, Edward Elgar.

Keil, R. and Lieser, P. (1992) 'Frankfurt: global city – local politics'. *Comparative Urban and Community Research* 4: 39-69.

Lake, R. (ed.) (1987) *Resolving Locational Conflict.* New Brunswick, NJ, Center for Urban Policy Research, Rutgers University.

Langton, S. (1978) 'What is Citizen Participation?'. Langton, S. (ed.) *Citizen Participation in America.* Lexingham Books, Lexingham, Mass.

Leyshon, A. and Thrift, N. (1989) 'South goes north? The rise of the British provincial financial centre'. In Lewis, J. and Townsend, A. (eds.) *The North-South Divide. Regional Change in Britain in the 1980s.* London: Paul Chapman.

Lloyd, M. and Newlands, D. (1988) 'The "growth coalition" and urban economic development'. *Local Economy* 3(1): 31-39.

Logan, J. (1978) 'Growth, Politics and the Stratification of Places'. *American Journal of Sociology* 84: 404-415.

Logan, J. and Molotch, H. (1987) *Urban Fortunes. The Political Economy of Place.* University of California Press.

Lowe, S. (1986) *Urban Social Movements.* The City After Castells. London, Macmillan.

MacDonald, G. (1994) 'Success of plan lead depends on monitors'. *Planning* No.1052, 21 January, pp.8-9.

Mény, Y. (1983) 'Permanence and change: the relations between central government and authorities in France'. *Environment and Planning C* 1: 17-28.

Molotch, H. (1979) 'Capital and Neighbourhood in the United States'. *Urban Affairs Quarterly* 14 (3): 298-312.

Molotch, H. and Logan, J. (1984) 'Tensions in the growth machine: overcoming resistance to value-free development'. *Social Problems* 31: 483-499.

Molotch, H and Logan, J. (1985) 'Urban Dependencies: new forms of use and exchange in US Cities'. *Urban Affairs Quarterly* 21: 143-169.

Molotch, H. and Vicari, S. (1988) 'Three ways to build: the development process in the US, Japan and Italy'. *Urban Affairs Quarterly* 24(2): 48-69.

Nadin, V. (1992) 'Local planning: progress and prospects'. *Planning Practice and Research* 7(3), pp.27-32.

Newman, P. (1994) 'Urban regime theory and comparative urban politics'. Paper presented at the conference on Cities, Enterprises and Society at the Eve of the XXIst Century, IFRESI, PIR Villes, Lille.

Peterson, P. (1987) *City Limits.* Chicago, University of Chicago Press.

Piven, F. and Friedland, R. (1984) 'Public choice and private power: a theory of fiscal crisis'. In Kirby,A., Knox, P. and Pinch, S. (eds) *Public Service Provision and Urban Development.* London, Croom Helm.

Potter, C., Anderson, M. and Meaton, J. (1994) 'Playing the planner – public participation in the urban fringe'. *Town and Country Planning* 63(2), pp.48-49.

Pratt, G. (1989) 'Incorporation Theory and The Production of Community Fabric' in Woles, J. and Dear, M. (1989) *The Power of Geography,* Unwin Hyman, London

Punter, J. (1989) 'France'. In Davies, H., Edwards, D., Hooper, A. and Punter, J. (eds) *Planning Control in Western Europe.* London, HMSO.

Purdue, M. (1994) 'THe impact of Section 54A'. *Journal of Planning and Environment Law* May: 399-407.

RCB (1990) Towards 2000. *Shaping the Future of Berkshire.* Reading, Royal County of Berkshire, Department of Highways and Planning.

Rhodes, R. (1986) *The National World of Local Government.* London, Allen and Unwin.

Rhodes, R. and Marsh, D. (1992a) 'Policy networks in British politics – a critique of existing approaches'. Chapter 1 in Marsh, D. and Rhodes, R. *Policy Networks in British Government.* Oxford, Clarendon Press.

Rhodes, R. and Marsh, D. (1992b) 'Policy communities and issue networks. Beyond typology'. Chapter 11 in Marsh, D. and Rhodes, R. *Policy Networks in British Government.* Oxford, Clarendon Press.

RTPI (1982) 'The Public and Planning: Means to Better Participation', Final Report of the Public Participation Working Party, London, Royal Town Planners Institute.

Shaw, K. (1993) 'The development of a new urban corporatism: the politics of urban regeneration in the north east of England'. *Regional Studies* 27(3), pp.251-259.

Short, J., Witt, A. and Fleming, S. (1986) *Housebuilding, Planning and Community Action. The Production and Negotiation of the Built Environment.* London, Routledge.

Simmie, J. (1981) *Power, Property and Corporatism.* Basingstoke, Macmillan.

Smith, A., Williams, G. and Houlder, M. (1986) 'Community influence on local planning policy'. *Progress in Planning* 25: 1-82.

Stone, C. (1976) *Economic Growth and Neighbourhood Discontent.* Raleigh, University of North Carolina Press.

Stone, C. (1989) *Regime Politics. Governing Atlanta 1946-1988.* Lawrence, Kansas, University of Kansas Press.

Stone, C., Orr, M., and Imbroscio, D. (1991) 'The reshaping of urban leadership in US cities: a regime analysis'. In Gottdiener, M. and Pickvance, C. (eds) *Urban Life in Transition.* London, Sage.

Sullivan, A. (1985) *Greening the Tories – New Policies on the Environment,* Centre for Policy Studies.

Thompson, R. (1991) 'The needs of industry'. Paper presented at conference on 'The Thames Valley and Western Corridor. What Future for the Quality of Life?'. Sponsored by Campbell Gordon and the Town and Country Planning Association.

Thornley, A. (1991) *Urban Planning Under Thatcherism. The Challenge of the Market.* London, Routledge.

Vicari, S. and Molotch, H. (1990) 'Building Milan: alternative machines of growth'. *International Journal of Urban and Regional Research* 14(4): 602-624.

Walker, R. (1981) 'A theory of suburbanisation: capitalism and the construction of urban space in the US'. In M. Dear and A. Scott (eds) *Urbanization and Urban Planning in Capitalist Society.* New York, Methuen.

Webster, B. and Lavers, A. (1991) 'The effectiveness of public local inquiries as a vehicle for public participation in the plan making process: a case study of the Barnet Unitary Development Plan inquiry'. *Journal of Planning and Environment Law,* pp.803-813.

Wilcox, D. (1994a) *The Guide to Effective Participation.* Brighton, Partnership Books.

Wilcox, D. (1994b) 'Participation – sham or shambles?'. *Planning* No. 1074, 24 June, p.7.

Appendix 1

The British, French and Swedish high-growth regions

Background

The case-study areas (see Figure 1) were chosen to be as similar as possible in analytical terms. Taking the Swedish case-study area first, between 1980 and 1987 employment grew by 139 per cent in the three communes which formed the core economic-growth zone (Sigtuna, Sollentuna, Upplands-Väsby, together with Kista parish in Stockholm commune). Incomes were 19 per cent over the Swedish average in 1985. Over three-quarters of the workforce from this zone lived in these or five neighbouring communes (Danderyd, Solna, Sundbyberg, Täby, Vallentuna). The remainder were more widely distributed in the Stockholm region or beyond. The population of this wider commuting zone grew by 10.4 per cent between 1975-87, compared to 5.7 per cent for the rest of Greater Stockholm. By 1987, 357,000 people lived there.

In Britain, the emergence of Berkshire as a key part of the 'M4 Corridor' or the 'Western Crescent' has been well-documented (for example, Hall et al. 1987). Although employment growth was much less dramatic than in the E4 Corridor, with a mere 6 per cent increase over the period, this started from a larger base. According to Hall et al (1987), during the late 1970s Berkshire saw the largest absolute growth in 'high-tech' jobs for any county. The trend in expansion in these sectors continued during the 1980s. Another growth sector was in financial and professional services: in 1984 Reading was the second largest sub-regional centre for all producer service employment and seventh largest for financial service jobs (Leyshon and Thrift 1989). The total population of Berkshire increased substantially during the 1970s and 1980s, from 631,000 (1971) to 718,000 in 1987. Net migration to the county grew during the 1980s, reaching approximately 3,000 new residents per annum.

Two French case-study areas were used in the analysis in order to capture the differences between a region where it was known that a relatively coherent 'growth coalition' existed (Toulouse) and one which was experiencing a pattern of development which was more directed by central and regional government (South Paris). In addition, an asymmetry existed between Toulouse and the British and Swedish case-study areas, inasmuch that both Berkshire and the E4 Corridor are closely influenced by their involvement in the London and Stockholm metropolitan regions, while Toulouse is a free-standing provincial city.

Before the early 1960s Toulouse was essentially a regional administrative and commercial centre, with a limited manufacturing base. Since the 1960s, though, the city has seen fundamental changes to its economic and employment structure. Some commentators have argued that the Toulouse region can be characterised as a regional 'technopole' (Galliano 1987; Galliano and Gilly 1987). The metropolitan area is the centre of the French aerospace industry and has also seen considerable growth in the computer, biotechnology and other 'high-tech' industries. The city's dynamic economy has led to rapid population growth, averaging around 5,000 new inhabitants per annum during the 1970s and early 1980s. By the end of the decade greater Toulouse's population was over 600,000, having increased by 15 per cent since 1975 (compared to a French national average of 4.3 per cent).

The South Paris area was delimited using employment and commuting data, and covers a number of communes in the *départements* of Essonne and Yvelines. Its total population was 1,735,000 in 1990. The area comprises three distinct zones, centred on the new towns of Evry and St. Quentin-en-Yvelines, and a group of communes around the towns of Massy, Saclay and Palaiseau. Total employment had grown by over 20 per cent during the 1980s, with particularly rapid growth in the pharmaceuticals, financial services, and electronics and electrical engineering sectors. Population growth was slower, rising by only 9 per cent during the period 1975-90. However, the two new towns saw much faster growth – St. Quentin-en-Yvelines grew by 55 per cent, and Evry by 19 per cent, during this period.

Similarities and differences between the case-study areas

Urban development pressure

All four case-study areas have seen high rates of housing development. In the largest, South Paris, between 5,000 and 7,000 units were completed each year during the 1980s, compared to between 2,000 and 4,000 in the E4 Corridor. Typical annual completions in Toulouse were between 4,000 and 5,000, but in the peak year (1988) 7,000 new dwellings – up to South Paris levels – were built. In Berkshire, on the other hand, completion rates of between 4,000 and 6,000 in the mid 1980s fell to only 2,000 units by the end of the decade. This bought absolute building levels well below E4 Corridor rates, an area of only half Berkshire's population.

While absolute numbers of housing completions are important, the housebuilding rate per capita may be taken as an indication of 'development pressure' on the local population. Table A1 shows this for the four growth areas. In all cases, apart from South Paris, per capita rates were high compared to the respective national average. The E4 Corridor, for example, displayed the highest rate of all, at an average of 7.3 new dwellings per 1000 population during the 1980s, compared to a Swedish average of 4.4. Toulouse saw the second highest rate, although Berkshire's rate was similar. The per capita rate in South Paris was much lower, at 3.6 per 1000, but it should be emphasised that this reflects the large population of this case-study area and the fact that it includes tracts of inner suburban housing with little new construction. As we have indicated, absolute housebuilding levels in South Paris were high: between 1984 and 1989 almost 35,000 dwellings were completed, representing about 15 per cent of the total for the whole of the Ile de France region. In addition, the bulk of new construction – 80 per cent of the area's total housebuilding in 1989 – was concentrated in Massy-Saclay-Palaiseau, where total annual completions rose from around 2,000 in 1982 to 5,000 by 1989. The per capita figures for this zone were therefore much higher than those for South Paris as a whole.

Table A1   Per capita housebuilding rates: growth areas compared to national average

Per capita housebuilding rate, average for 1980s (dwellings per 1000 population)

	Growth area	National average
E4 Corridor	7.3	4.4
Toulouse	6.8	4.6
Berkshire	6.1	3.1
South Paris	3.6	4.4

Source: local and national statistics

In Chapter 1 we suggested that anti-development protest may partly be influenced by levels of home ownership, with residents being concerned to

Figure A1 Tenure diversity in new housing: the high-growth regions, 1980-1989

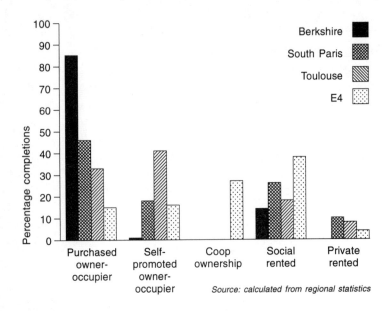

Source: calculated from regional statistics

defend their localities against urban development because of anxiety over its effects on house prices. Existing differences in the tenurial structure of the housing stock in the case-study areas were reinforced in the 1980s by new construction. Figure A1 shows that almost all housing built in the 1980s in Berkshire was for purchase by owner-occupiers, with just 14 per cent in social renting. In the E4 Corridor, on the other hand, social renting was the leading tenure, accounting for 38 per cent of new build over the decade. The two French areas also showed greater diversity than Berkshire. Although there was a significant social rented sector in both the Toulouse area and South Paris, the emphasis in both areas was on owner-occupation.

It is hard to compare house-price levels in the case-study areas because of differences in the way national and local statistics measure this information (see Barlow and Duncan 1992; 1994). Taking the sales prices of new owner-occupier housing as a measure,[1] it is clear that absolute house prices varied markedly. Comparing prices on a purchasing power parity basis (thereby providing a closer indication of comparative costs to the consumer), the average newly-built dwelling in Berkshire cost around £80,000 in 1989. This was about 17 per cent higher than the E4 Corridor, 22 per cent higher than South Paris and 60 per cent higher than Toulouse. In Berkshire very steep real price increases in the mid 1980s were followed by a slump at the end of the decade; South Paris also experienced a steep

Figure A2   Final output costs: the high-growth regions, 1980-1989

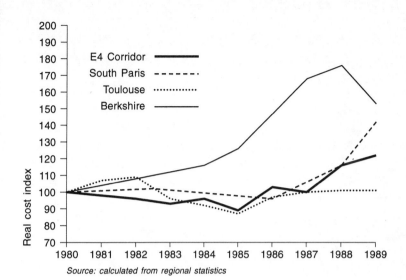

Source: calculated from regional statistics

price rise in the late 1980s. Toulouse and the E4 Corridor experienced more stable price trends, with real declines until the late 1980s, although there was inflation in the E4 Corridor costs at the end of the decade (see Figure A2).

As well as the level of housebuilding, another indicator of local growth pressure, with possibly significant implications for the perceptions of local residents about the amount new urban growth, is the amount of land sold for housing development.[2] Some of this land is for immediate development and some is for longer term speculative investment. During the 1980s there were sharp up- and down-swings in the amount of land traded in Berkshire. The early 1980s, for example, was marked by a massive increase in sales of land and a large rise in housing completions. By 1984, however, land sales were falling, with a decline in completions in the following year. There was another surge in land sales in 1986, but this time completions only increased slightly. Subsequently, land sales and completions fell dramatically as the recession in the housing market began to bite.

Details are not available for South Paris, but in Toulouse there were also significant variations in the amount of development land traded annually. During there early 1980s there was a sharp fall in land sales,. There was then a surge in land sales and completions, followed by a period of relatively stable land sales and falling completions. However, a sudden upturn in housebuilding occurred in 1987 – housing completions grew by

45 per cent in one year and 62 per cent in the following year. Land trading took off again in 1988 and continued at a high level until the end of the decade.

Figures for the E4 Corridor show that the amount of land traded for housing development grew massively during the early 1980s and stabilised for the remainder of the decade.

Local government systems

As we noted in Chapter 1, there are differences between the three countries in the relative financial and decision-making autonomy of local government *vis-à-vis* the national government. These differences are reflected in the local government structures of the case-study areas.

Swedish local authorities have a high level of political autonomy and considerable fiscal powers. This includes a local income tax, the ability to purchase land for publicly-owned housing development land banks and an obligation to formulate detailed local five-year housebuilding plans for their area. While this is the case for the nine communes of the E4 Corridor, to some extent policies established at a metropolitan and national level set the broad parameters for housing development during the mid-to-late-1980s. Regional planning authorities for Stockholm established broad indicative plans and in 1986 a 'Housing Delegation' *(Bostadsdelegation)* was set up by national government to tackle the housing shortage perceived in Stockholm County. This recommended limits on commercial building and a balance between office development space and housing space.

The situation is completely different in Britain, although the surface pattern of local government is similar. In Berkshire six district councils have powers to grant planning permission, and responsibility for the formulation of local plans. Berkshire County Council is responsible for broad strategic planning, but there is no mechanism for ensuring coordination between county councils at the regional level. Nor have British local authorities ever had the political and financial autonomy of their Swedish counterparts, having been more subject to centrally imposed political and fiscal authority. During the 1980s local autonomy was reduced even further (Duncan and Goodwin 1987), such that even the National Audit Office concluded that by 1993 local government powers were 'largely cosmetic' *(The Guardian,* 20 March 1993).

The French local government system is different again. Historically a centralised system, the accent during the 1970s and 1980s was on decentralisation. However, despite the introduction of a regional tier of government, coordination between local planning authorities is relatively poor because of the fragmentation of the system into a large number of small communes, which retain considerable autonomy in urban planning. The government therefore encouraged communes to group themselves into associations for urban planning and development purposes. A variety of different forms of association were introduced in the 1980s, with varying degrees of decision-making power.[3] The functional and legal relationships within which associations are situated are frequently complex, involving agreements with *départements* and the regional authority, and the establishment of mixed public-private bodies to implement development schemes.

The South Paris study area consists of 82 communes, split between two *départements*. In addition the area includes two new towns (Evry and St Quentin-en-Yvelines). A number of communes have been regrouped into various types of association for planning purposes. Some of these have the power to harmonise and redistribute local business taxes.

The Toulouse metropolitan area is dominated by the city itself, with 60 per cent of the total population. The remaining surrounding area is split into 61 communes. There are three important groupings of communes in greater Toulouse. Apart from the Toulouse commune itself, which accounts for about half the conurbation's population, there is an association of communes which aims to create growth pole in the western suburbs and a large association based around the south-eastern suburban communes. In the case of the latter, the Toulouse strategic plan area cuts across the boundaries.

Notes
1. In the French and British case-study areas this is the predominant means of acquiring newly-built housing, although around 20 per cent of new housing is for rent in the French examples. In the E4 Corridor only 16 per cent of new housing built in the 1980s was sold by developers for owner-occupation (and another 18 per cent was self-built). Here we used a composite measure reflecting cost levels for all new housing output, including rental, cooperative and owner-occupied housing. This is based on the final production cost for new housing which, given the price controls on new output in the state housing-loan system, is effectively the same as the final consumer price.
2. See Barlow (1993) and Barlow and Duncan (1994) for further details of the land markets in the case-study areas.
3. These include: *établissement public, syndicat intercommunal* and *district intercommunal*. The latter provide a more binding form of contract between communes. The government is currently discussing possible ways of simplifying inter-communal arrangements.

Appendix 2

Case-study areas: Research method

The research involved the following tasks:

- Building up a planning history of the case-study area, including the assessment of local and regional plans, other relevant planning documents, and documentation relating to major development proposals.

- Interviews with planning authorities, other statutory planning bodies, employers' federations, developers and developers' federations, residents' groups. These were to provide a broad overview of planning practice in the case-study areas and to test some of the preliminary findings of the research.

- Analysis of public submissions and representations regarding local plans and development applications, to examine the type of issues attracting public attention, the main groups involved in participation, and the point in the development process when intervention was made.

- Analysis of planning application success rates (see Appendix 3). The objective was to examine whether applications are more likely to be refused consent under the British approach than under a legally-binding zoning or public land-banking system.

We encountered some problems in surveying local employers. A sample survey of firms in Berkshire received a poor response, probably because the recession has made employers less concerned about urban-development issues. We therefore decided it was more cost-effective in the other case-study areas to obtain a broad overview by interviewing local employers federations and examining written submissions made by local firms about planning issues. Some interviews with firms which had made submissions were also carried out.

There was also a problem of availability of data on planning applications. While this data was easily obtained for the British and French case-study areas, records were not readily available for the E4 Corridor. Apart from this, all other data collection and interviews were successful.

Appendix 3

Data on planning applications in the British and French case-study areas

Table A1 Planning applications in Toulouse metropolitan area

Yyear	permitted	withdrawn	refused	undecided	Total	% refused
1980	1,969	58	0	0	2,027	0.0
1981	2,213	132	0	0	2,345	0.0
1982	2,481	81	0	0	2,562	0.0
1983	2,486	130	0	0	2,616	0.0
1984	2,630	30	1	0	2,661	0.0
1985	2,767	189	0	0	2,956	0.0
1986	2,875	186	1	0	3,062	0.0
1987	3,242	264	1	0	3,507	0.0
1988	3,386	445	0	0	3,831	0.0
1989	6,888	298	475	0	7,661	6.2
1990-91	13,868	1,082	458	9	15,417	3.0

Source: Direction Départemental de l'Equipement

Table A2   Planning applications in South Paris

Year	Permitted	Withdrawn	Refused	Undecided	Total	% refused
1986	7749	261	358	25	8393	4.3
1987	8981	249	452	13	9695	4.7
1988	8769	234	430	16	9449	4.6
1989	6219	206	385	26	6836	5.6
1990	8191	220	614	45	9070	6.8
1991	7286	286	563	24	8159	6.9

Source: Direction Régional de l'Equipement

Table A3   Planning applications in selected Berkshire districts*

Year	Permitted	Withdrawn	Refused	Total	% refused
1981	537	42	351	930	37.7
1982	497	30	327	854	38.3
1983	552	34	307	893	34.4
1984	511	40	339	890	38.1
1985	590	44	339	973	34.8
1986	638	44	382	1064	35.9
1987	665	79	417	1161	35.9
1988	475	85	544	1104	49.3
1989	452	34	236	722	32.7
1990	382	28	172	582	29.6
1991	312	16	128	456	28.1
1992	310	13	97	420	23.1

Source: Berkshire County Council

Number of undecided applications not available

*   Bracknell, Newbury, Wokingham

Index